Wisdom from the Monastery

Wisdom from the Monastery

*The Rule of St Benedict
for everyday life*

LITURGICAL PRESS
Collegeville, Minnesota

www.litpress.org

© the Contributors 2003, 2005

The Rule of St Benedict © Ampleforth Abbey Trustees 1997

Wisdom from the Monastery is an extract
from *The Benedictine Handbook*

First published in 2005 by the Canterbury Press Norwich
(a publishing imprint of Hymns Ancient & Modern Limited,
a registered charity)
St Mary's Works, St Mary's Plain,
Norwich, Norfolk, NR3 3BH

www.scm-canterburypress.co.uk

Published in the United States of America and Canada by Liturgical Press,
Saint John's Abbey, Collegeville, Minnesota 56321-7500

www.litpress.org

ISBN 0-8146-3153-3

Contents

Introduction

When St Benedict of Nursia put down his pen some time in the sixth century, he had completed one of the most remarkable and long-lasting achievements of his and any other century. Since his time, there have been men and women committed to the search for God that he describes, a search that has always been shared with oblates, friends, pilgrims and visitors who have come to Benedict's monasteries since the beginning. This handbook is one expression of that ongoing sharing.

Most people coming to a monastery for the first time have one question at the back of their minds: 'What do you, the monks or nuns, actually do?' This is not a bad question with which to approach the heart of the Benedictine life – let me give an example.

In 1309, two rather dishevelled monks were summoned to answer exactly this question. It was not, at the beginning, a friendly encounter.

On the one side were three busy officials of the King of England, Edward I. They had been sent to the last remaining fragments of the King's regions in France, and specifically to the island of Jersey, to enquire into the state of Royal property. Facing them were two monks, by birth loyal to the King of France, by monastic vow attached to a Norman monastery and by chance of appointment abandoned on a remote outcrop of rock between Jersey and the Cherbourg peninsula. Their rock was truly tiny – at high tide little more than a break in the waves – but the King of England was nevertheless interested in who owned it, and, more particularly, in what its only two residents did. Their answer is recorded in the plain style of a legal document:

> 'He who is called Prior and his companion . . . dwelling in the chapel throughout the whole year maintain a light burning in that chapel so that the sailors crossing the sea by that light may avoid the peril of the reef . . . where the greatest danger exists of being wrecked. These two always perform the divine office.'

To me, this simple answer reveals much about the nature of the Benedictine vocation. In so many different ways throughout its history, and in so many different places throughout the world today, Benedictine women and men have engaged in precisely that same task of bearing a light that shines not for their own glory but for the good of the church and the world. So the aim of this book is very simple – to be a support to those many people who come into contact with monasteries today and who want to deepen their experience of the monastic way in their own lives. You may live under the shadow of some mighty monastery, or you may be a visitor who has always wondered whether such places still exist. You may be an oblate or supporter of a new foundation, or you may live a long way from a monastery such that you want to take a part of it with you. If you belong to any one of these groups, then this book is for you.

It is not written for monks and nuns themselves, but rather for those who belong, in whatever sense, to the wider family of the Benedictines. It is not meant to be read all at once – we hope that you will dip in and out of it, sometimes for information but more often for support in prayer and for deepening your own sense of belonging.

The handbook starts, in Part One, with Benedict's own Rule, the foundation charter for the ongoing experience of monasticism in the Latin churches. Though enriched over the centuries by commentaries and interpretations of every sort, the Rule must always stand alone, for it is to St Benedict's timeless wisdom that all those who take his name must return. It is the basis for everything else that follows, and what follows will, we hope, lead you back to Benedict, and through him to the Gospel of Christ which is Benedict's inspiration. It is a short document, and a mixture of the spiritual and the practical, just as our lives are called to become.

Part Two explores the tools of monastic life, the particular activities which shape the son or daughter of St Benedict and his or her relation to the world.

Wherever you are within the Benedictine world, it is the aim of this and the larger book, *The Benedictive Handbook* from which *Wisdom from the Monastery* is extracted, that you might feel that you belong there. It is the prayer of all of those who have been involved with this book that, with its help, you may continue 'to prefer nothing whatever to Christ'.

Fr Anthony Marett-Crosby OSB
Ampleforth Abbey

About the Contributors

Patrick Barry OSB was born in England in 1917. He became a monk of Ampleforth Abbey in 1936 and was ordained priest in 1945. He was Headmaster of Ampleforth College for fifteen years and Abbot of the Abbey from 1984 to 1997.

Michael Casey OCSO is a monk of Tarrawarra Abbey, Australia. He is involved in the formation of his own community and other monastic communities internationally. He is the author of several books on monastic spirituality.

Demetrius R. Dumm OSB is a monk of St Vincent Archabbey, Latrobe, Pennsylvania, a professor of the New Testament in St Vincent Seminary, and the author of several books, including *Cherish Christ Above All: The Bible in the Rule of St Benedict.*

Mary Forman OSB is a member of the Monastery of St Gertrude, Cottonwood, Idaho. She teaches monastic studies at the School of Theology·Seminary, St John's University, Collegeville, Minnesota.

Kym Harris OSB is a nun of the Monastery of Transfiguration at Yeppoon in Central Queensland, Australia. She has worked in various areas in her monastic life, primarily in crafts like pottery, leather work and candle decoration. She was editor of *Tjurunga: The Australasian Benedictine Review* for five years. In 1996 she received a Master's Degree from the Melbourne College of

Divinity for a thesis on the spirituality of the medieval monastic women. She is a keen gardener.

Laurence McTaggart grew up in Nottingham where his parents were doctors. In 1991 he became a monk of Ampleforth Abbey where he enjoys teaching in the monastic school, giving retreats, playing the organ and picking apples.

Kathleen Norris is the author of four memoirs, *Dakota: A Spiritual Geography*, *The Cloister Walk*, *Amazing Grace: A Vocabulary of Faith*, and *The Virgin of Bennington*, and several volumes of poetry. She has been an oblate of Assumption Abbey, Richardton, North Dakota, since 1986.

Richard Yeo OSB is Abbot of Downside and Abbot President of the English Benedictine Congregation. Born in 1948, he became a monk of Downside in 1970. Studies in Rome included work on the structure and content of the monastic profession. Before becoming Abbot, he worked in the Vatican office dealing with religious orders.

Part One

Saint Benedict's Rule

A Short Introduction

It may seem extravagant today to suggest that not only monks and nuns but also ordinary laymen and laywomen of the twenty-first century can learn something invaluable about themselves and about how to live their lives on this earth by reading what St Benedict wrote in the sixth century and by taking it to heart. Yet in considering that strange proposition we might start by looking at the actual use of the Rule throughout the ages, and reflecting that it has been alive and active through all the centuries that have elapsed since it was written. During all that time it has provided spiritual inspiration to countless monks and nuns in their desire to dedicate their whole being to God. During all that time it has also stretched out beyond the walls of the monasteries. It has given spiritual inspiration and encouragement to many of the laity who have been associated as oblates with Benedictine abbeys throughout the world. And now in this present age it has gone even further than that.

Since the Second Vatican Council the Rule has acquired a new lease of life among the laity. There have been young lay movements in the Church that have adopted St Benedict's Rule to provide them with structure and guidance in their way of life. There have been lay groups at parochial and national level who have found in it much of the spiritual inspiration that they seek in their desire to lead lay lives in more faithful service of Christ and of their fellow men and women. There have been groups in other Churches, Anglican, Episcopalian, Protestant, who have recognized in the Rule a seminal document from the days before the schisms and sad divisions of Christianity and find in it a source of spirituality untainted by the rancour of division. There are Buddhists in open, peaceful dialogue with Christianity who have found in the Rule of St Benedict echoes, affirmations and analogies which correspond with something in their own search for self-understanding, for community, for harmony and for ultimate meaning in their journey of life. All this evidence of a new life for the Rule among the laity is no dream but solid fact of what has actually already happened. It raises the deep and interesting question about what it is in the Rule that can span the centuries in this way and still provide spiritual inspiration for the future.

The Rule was written by St Benedict for his monks to guide them in their search for God through their life of dedication. Whatever the sources and influences that went into its creation, it has a simplicity and directness of appeal which is still power-ful. It is without pretension and is written in the rough, common Latin of the time, which is far from the polished sonority of classical Latin but which has a deeply attractive rhythm of its own. St Benedict had an ear for the music of words. He also had an insight into the hearts of human beings in their search for self-knowledge and truth and meaning in life. There are parts of the Rule which are simply regulations, so necessary to make community life harmonious and possible. There are parts which are disciplinary, which are there – in Benedict's own words – because they are 'demanded reasonably for the correction of vice and the preservation of love'.[1] Yet, even when he is dealing with the control of real wickedness, it is never stern regulations that matter to him but the ultimate supremacy of prayer and love. Thus he recommends that, when all other means have failed to correct wrongdoing, the abbot should turn to some-thing 'which is still more powerful' than any disciplinary measures, 'namely the personal prayer of the superior and of all the community that the Lord, who can do all things, may himself bring healing to the delinquent'.[2]

The real heart of the Rule, however, and the power which has kept it alive and relevant to Christian life today is not the regulations and practical directions for community living, valuable though they are. The heart of the Rule is in the chapters of spiritual guidance which are so full of the timeless wisdom of scripture. Outstanding among these are the Prologue, Chapter 4 on guidelines for Christian living, Chapter 7 on humility, the chapters of guidance for the abbot in the exercise of authority and Chapter 72, which in a few short sentences summarizes the whole spirit of the Rule. In these chapters and in many other passages which could be quoted, St Benedict writes as though speaking in intimate dialogue with a young aspirant who is seeking his advice. His manner, and his very words, are couched in this vein so that he seems even to be offering himself more as a spiritual companion than as a masterful leader in the journey of life. He achieves this through reflections of great depth on our relationships with our creator, our redeemer, on our use of the world we live in, on our interaction with each other, on our considered assessment of ourselves and our place in the universe, on freedom from vice and egomania, on our search for a peace and a fulfilment which is free from arrogance, greed, anger and all that disturbs the inner tranquility of 'that love of God which in its fullness casts out all fear'.[3]

There is one other point to be made and it is perhaps the most important of all. St Benedict does not speak on his own authority. He is personally formed on the word of God in scripture and his language is shot through with scriptural phrases and concepts. Even when he is not actually quoting scripture there is usually a scriptural echo in his words. The whole power of the Rule, then, comes from the word of scripture and that is what makes its message timeless, participating, as it does, in the richness of the word of scripture which is ever old and ever new.

A Note on the Text

In the Latin text of the Rule the sentences in each chapter have been numbered. This may sometimes be a help to scholarly study. This translation, however, is intended to be read holistically as an experience of sacred reading which is close to prayer or meditation. References can nevertheless be made to it by chapter and paragraph. Where references to the text have been made in this book they have followed that pattern.

Patrick Barry OSB

Notes

1 See Prologue, last paragraph.
2 See Chapter 28.
3 See Chapter 7, last paragraph.

Saint Benedict's Rule

A New Translation for Today

Patrick Barry OSB

CONTENTS

Prologue to The Rule

LISTEN, CHILD OF GOD, TO THE GUIDANCE OF YOUR
teacher. Attend to the message you hear and make sure that
it pierces to your heart, so that you may accept with willing
freedom and fulfil by the way you live the directions that
come from your loving Father. It is not easy to accept and
persevere in obedience, but it is the way to return to Christ,
when you have strayed through the laxity and carelessness
of disobedience. My words are addressed to you especially,
whoever you may be, whatever your circumstances, who
turn from the pursuit of your own self-will and ask to
enlist under Christ, who is Lord of all, by following him
through taking to yourself that strong and blessed armour
of obedience which he made his own on coming into our
world.

This, then, is the beginning of my advice: make prayer the
first step in anything worthwhile that you attempt.
Persevere and do not weaken in that prayer. Pray with
confidence, because God, in his love and forgiveness, has
counted us as his own sons and daughters. Surely we
should not by our evil acts heartlessly reject that love.
At every moment of our lives, as we use the good things
he has given us, we can respond to his love only by
seeking to obey his will for us. If we should refuse, what
wonder to find ourselves disinherited! What wonder if he,
confronted and repelled by the evil in us, should abandon
us like malicious and rebellious subjects to the never-

ending pain of separation since we refused to follow Him to glory.

However late, then, it may seem, let us rouse ourselves from lethargy. That is what scripture urges on us when it says: the time has come for us to rouse ourselves from sleep.[1] Let us open our eyes to the light that can change us into the likeness of God. Let our ears be alert to the stirring call of his voice crying to us every day: today, if you should hear his voice, do not harden your hearts.[2] And again: let anyone with ears to hear listen to what the Spirit says to the churches.[3] And this is what the Spirit says: Come my children, hear me, and I shall teach you the fear of the Lord.[4] Run, while you have the light of life, before the darkness of death overtakes you.[5]

It is to find workers in his cause that God calls out like that to all peoples. He calls to us in another way in the psalm when he says: Who is there with a love of true life and a longing for days of real fulfilment?[6] If you should hear that call and answer: 'I', this is the answer you will receive from God: If you wish to have that true life that lasts for ever, then keep your tongue from evil; let your lips speak no deceit; turn away from wrongdoing; seek out peace and pursue it.[7] If you do that, he says, I shall look on you with such love and my ears will be so alert to your prayer that, before you so much as call on me, I shall say to you: here I am.[8] What gentler encouragement could we have, my dear brothers and sisters, than that word from the Lord calling us to himself in such a way! We can see with what loving concern the Lord points out to us the path of life.

And so to prepare ourselves for the journey before us let us renew our faith and set ourselves high standards by which to lead our lives. The gospel should be our guide in following the way of Christ to prepare ourselves for his presence in the kingdom to which he has called us. If we want to make our lasting home in his holy kingdom, the only way is to set aright the course of our lives in doing what is good. We should make our own the psalmist's question: Lord, who will dwell in your kingdom or who will find rest on your holy mountain?[9] In reply we may hear from the same psalmist the Lord's answer to show us the way that leads to his kingdom: anyone who leads a life without guile, who does what is right, who speaks truth from the heart, on whose tongue there is no deceit, who never harms a neighbour nor believes evil reports about another,[10] who at once rejects outright from the heart the devil's temptations to sin, destroying them utterly at the first onset by casting them before Christ himself.[11] Such a follower of Christ lives in reverence of him and does not take the credit for a good life but, believing that all the good we do comes from the Lord, gives him the credit and thanksgiving for what his gift brings about in our hearts. In that spirit our prayer from the psalm should be: not to us, O Lord, not to us give the glory but to your own name.[12] That is St Paul's example, for he took no credit to himself for his preaching when he said: it is by God's grace that I am what I am.[13] And again he says: Let anyone who wants to boast, boast in the Lord.[14]

The Lord himself in the gospel teaches us the same when he says: I shall liken anyone who hears my words and carries them out in deed to one who is wise enough to build on a rock; then the floods came and the winds blew and struck that house, but it did not fall because it was built on a rock.[15] It is in the light of that teaching that the Lord waits for us every day to see if we will respond by our deeds, as we should, to his holy guidance. For that very reason also, so that we may mend our evil ways, the days of our mortal lives are allowed us as a sort of truce for improvement. So St Paul says: Do you not know that God is patient with us so as to lead us to repentance?[16] The Lord himself says in his gentle care for us: I do not want the death of a sinner; let all sinners rather turn away from sin and live.[17]

Well then, brothers and sisters, we have questioned the Lord about who can dwell with him in his holy place and we have heard the demands he makes on such a one; we can be united with him there, only if we fulfil those demands. We must, therefore, prepare our hearts and bodies to serve him under the guidance of holy obedience. Conscious in this undertaking of our own weakness let us ask the Lord to give us through his grace the help we need. If we want to avoid the pain of self-destruction in hell and come to eternal life, then, while we still have the time in this mortal life and the opportunity to fulfil what God asks of us through a life guided by his light, we must hurry forward and act in a way that will bring us blessings in eternal life.

With all this in mind what we mean to establish is a school for the Lord's service. In the guidance we lay down to achieve this we hope to impose nothing harsh or burdensome. If, however, you find in it anything which seems rather strict, but which is demanded reasonably for the correction of vice or the preservation of love, do not let that frighten you into fleeing from the way of salvation; it is a way which is bound to seem narrow to start with. But, as we progress in this monastic way of life and in faith, our hearts will warm to its vision and with eager love and delight that defies expression we shall go forward on the way of God's commandments. Then we shall never think of deserting his guidance; we shall persevere in fidelity to his teaching in the monastery until death so that through our patience we may be granted some part in Christ's own passion and thus in the end receive a share in his kingdom. Amen.

CHAPTER 1

Four approaches to monastic life

WE CAN ALL RECOGNIZE THE DISTINCTION BETWEEN the four different kinds of monk. First of all there are the cenobites. These are the ones who are based in a monastery and fulfil their service of the Lord under a rule and an abbot or abbess.

Anchorites, who are also known as hermits, are the second kind. Their vocation is not the result of the first fervour so often experienced by those who give themselves to a monastic way of life. On the contrary they have learnt well from everyday experience with the support of many others in a community how to fight against the devil. Thus they are well trained in the ranks of their brothers or sisters before they have the confidence to do without that support and venture into single combat in the desert relying only on their own arms and the help of God in their battle against the evil temptations of body and mind.

Sarabaites are the third kind of monk and the example they give of monasticism is appalling. They have been through no period of trial under a rule with the experienced guidance of a teacher, which might have proved them as gold is proved in a furnace. On the contrary they are as malleable as lead and their standards are still those of the secular world, so that it is clear to everyone that their tonsure is a lie before God himself. They go around in twos or threes, or even singly, resting in sheepfolds which are not those of the Lord, but which they make to suit themselves. For a rule of life they have only the satisfaction of their own desires. Any precept they think up for themselves and then decide to adopt they do not hesitate to call holy. Anything they dislike they consider inadmissible.

Finally those called gyrovagues are the fourth kind of monk. They spend their whole life going round one province after another enjoying the hospitality for three or four days at a time at any sort of monastic cell or community. They are always on the move; they never settle to put down the roots of stability; it is their own wills that they serve as they seek the satisfaction of their own gross appetites. They are in every way worse than the sarabaites.

About the wretched way of life that all these so-called monks pursue it is better to keep silence than to speak. Let us leave them to themselves and turn to the strongest kind, the cenobites, so that with the Lord's help we may consider the regulation of their way of life.

CHAPTER 2

Gifts needed by an abbot or abbess

ANYONE WHO ASPIRES AS ABBOT OR ABBESS TO BE superior of a monastery should always remember what is really meant by the title and fulfil in their monastic life all that is required in one holding the office of monastic superior. For it is the place of Christ that the superior is understood to hold in the monastery by having a name which belongs to Christ, as St Paul suggests when he writes: You have received the spirit of adopted children whereby we cry *abba*, Father.[1] That means that the abbot or abbess should never teach anything nor make any arrangement nor give any order which is against the teaching of the Lord. Far from it, everything he or she commands or teaches should be like a leaven of the holiness that comes from God infused into the minds of their disciples. In fact they should remember that they will have to account in the awesome judgement of God both for their own teaching and also for the obedience of their disciples. They should be well aware that the shepherd will have to bear the blame for any deficiency that God, as the Father of the whole human family, finds in his sheep. However, it is also true that, if the flock has been unruly and disobedient and the superiors have done everything possible as shepherds to cure their vicious ways, then they will be absolved in the judgement of God and may say with the psalmist: I have not hidden your teaching in my heart; I have proclaimed your truth and the salvation you offer, but they despised and rejected me.[2]

Any, then, who accept the name of abbot or abbess should give a lead to their disciples by two distinct methods of teaching – by the example of the lives they lead (and that is the most important way) and by the words they use in their teaching. To disciples who can understand they may teach the way of the Lord with words; but to the less receptive and uneducated they should teach what the Lord commands us by example. Of course, whenever they teach a disciple that something is wrong they should themselves show by the practical example they give that it must not be done. If they fail in this they themselves, although they have preached well to others, may be rejected and God may respond to their sinfulness by saying: Why do you repeat my teaching and take the words of my covenant on your lips, while you yourself have rejected my guidance and cast my words away?[3] And again: You noticed the speck of dust in your brother's eye but failed to see the beam in your own.[4]

They should not select for special treatment any individual
in the monastery. They should not love one more than
another unless it is for good observance of the Rule and
obedience. One who is free-born should not, for that
reason, be advanced before one coming to monastic life
from a condition of slavery, unless there is some other good
reason for it. If such a reason is seen by the abbot or
abbess to be justified they can decide on a change for any
member of the community. Otherwise all must keep their
proper place in the community order, because whether slave
or free we are all one in Christ and we owe an equal service in
the army of one Lord, who shows no special favour to one
rather than another.[5] The only grounds on which in Christ's
eyes one is to be preferred to another is by excelling in good
works and humility. The abbot or abbess, then, should show
equal love to all and apply the same standards of discipline to
all according to what they deserve.

They should make their own the different ways of teaching
which the Apostle Paul recommended to Timothy when he
told him to make use of criticism, of entreaty and of
rebuke.[6] Thus in adapting to changing circumstances they
should use now the encouragement of a loving parent and
now the threats of a harsh disciplinarian. This means that
they should criticize more sternly those who are
undisciplined and unruly; they should entreat those who are
obedient, docile and patient so as to encourage their
progress; but they should rebuke and punish those who
take a feckless attitude or show contempt for what they are
taught.

A monastic superior should never show tolerance of
wrongdoing, but as soon as it begins to grow should
root it out completely to avoid the dangerous error of Eli,
the priest of Shiloh.[7] Any who are reliable and able to
understand should be admonished by words on the first
and second occasion; but those who are defiant and

resistant in the pride of their disobedience will need to be corrected by corporal punishment at the very beginning of their evil course. It should be remembered that scripture says: a fool cannot be corrected by words alone;[8] and again: strike your child with a rod whose soul will by this means be saved from death.[9]

Reflection on their own high status in the monastery and the meaning of their title should be ever present to the abbot or abbess. This will make them aware of what is meant by the saying that more is demanded of those to whom more is entrusted.[10] They should reflect on what a difficult and demanding task they have accepted, namely that of guiding souls and serving the needs of so many different characters; gentle encouragement will be needed for one, strong rebukes for another, rational persuasion for another, according to the character and intelligence of each. It is the task of the superiors to adapt with sympathetic understanding to the needs of each so that they may not only avoid any loss but even have the joy of increasing the number of good sheep in the flock committed to them.

It is above all important that monastic superiors should not underrate or think lightly of the salvation of the souls committed to them by giving too much attention to transient affairs of this world which have no lasting value. They should remember always that the responsibility they have undertaken is that of guiding souls and that they will have to render an account of the guidance they have given. If resources are slender for the monastery they should remember this saying from scripture: seek first the kingdom of God and his righteousness and all these things will be given to you also;[11] then also there is the text: nothing is lacking for those who fear him.[12]

It should be very clear to superiors that all who undertake the guidance of souls must in the end prepare themselves to give an account of that guidance. However many the souls for whom they are responsible all superiors may be sure that they will be called to account before the Lord for each one of them and after that for their own souls as well. Frequent reverent reflection on that future reckoning before the Good Shepherd who has committed his sheep to them will, through their concern for others, inspire them to greater care of their own souls. By encouraging through their faithful ministry better standards for those in their care, they will develop higher ideals in their own lives as well.

※

CHAPTER 3

Calling the community together for consultation

When any business of importance is to be considered in the monastery, the abbot or abbess should summon the whole community together and personally explain to them the agenda that lies before them. After hearing the advice of the community, the superior should consider it carefully in private and only then make a judgement about what is the best decision. We have insisted that all the community should be summoned for such consultation, because it often happens that the Lord makes the best course clear to one of the youngest. The community themselves should be careful to offer their advice with due deference and respect, avoiding an obstinate defence of their own convictions. It is for the abbot or abbess in the end to make the decision and everyone else should obey what the superior judges to be best. To get the balance right it should be remembered that, whereas it is right for subordinates to obey their superior, it is just as important for the superior to be far-sighted and fair in administration.

Such an ideal can be achieved only if everyone duly conforms to the authority of the Rule and no one gives way to self-will by deviating from it. In a monastery no one should follow the prompting of what are merely personal desires nor should any monk or nun take it on themselves to oppose the abbot or abbess defiantly, especially in a public forum outside the monastery. Anyone who is rash enough to act in such a way should be disciplined in accordance with the Rule. However the superior should in everything personally keep the fear of God clearly in view and take care to act in accordance with the requirements of the Rule, while also remembering the future account of all such decisions to be rendered before the supremely just tribunal of the Lord.

What has been said about consultation so far, applies to matters of weight and importance. When questions of lesser concern arise in the monastery and call for a decision, the abbot or abbess should consult with seniors alone. Such is the appropriate way to conform to that precept of scripture: If you act always after hearing the counsel of others, you will avoid the need to repent of your decision afterwards.[1]

CHAPTER 4

Guidelines for Christian and monastic good practice

THE FIRST OF ALL THINGS TO AIM AT IS TO LOVE THE
Lord God with your whole heart and soul and strength and
then to love your neighbour as much as you do yourself.
The other commandments flow from these two: not to kill,
not to commit adultery, not to steal, not to indulge our
base desires, not to give false evidence against another, to
give due honour to all and not to inflict on someone else
what you would resent if it were done to yourself.

Renounce your own desires and ambitions so as to be free to
follow Christ. Control your body with self-discipline; don't
give yourself to unrestrained pleasure; learn to value the
self-restraint of fasting. Give help and support to the poor;
clothe the naked, visit the sick and bury the dead. Console
and counsel those who suffer in time of grief and bring
comfort to those in sorrow.

Don't get too involved in purely worldly affairs and count
nothing more important than the love you should cherish
for Christ. Don't let your actions be governed by anger nor
nurse your anger against a future opportunity of indulging
it. Don't harbour in your heart any trace of deceit nor
pretend to be at peace with another when you are not;
don't abandon the true standards of charity. Don't use
oaths to make your point for fear of perjury, but speak
the truth with integrity of heart and tongue.

If you are harmed by anyone, never repay it by returning the
harm. In fact you should never inflict any injury on another
but bear patiently whatever you have to suffer. Love your
enemies, then; refrain from speaking evil but rather call a

blessing on those who speak evil of you; if you are persecuted for favouring a just cause, then bear it patiently.

Avoid all pride and self-importance. Don't drink to excess nor over-eat. Don't be lazy nor give way to excessive sleep. Don't be a murmurer* and never in speaking take away the good name of another.

Your hope of fulfilment should be centred in God alone. When you see any good in yourself, then, don't take it to be your very own, but acknowledge it as a gift from God. On the other hand you may be sure that any evil you do is always your own and you may safely acknowledge your responsibility.

You should recognize that there will be a day of reckoning and judgement for all of us, which should make us afraid of how we stand between good and evil. But, while you should have a just fear of the loss of everything in hell, you should above all cultivate a longing for eternal life with a desire of great spiritual intensity. Keep the reality of death always before your eyes, have a care about how you act every hour of your life and be sure that God is present everywhere and that he certainly sees and understands what you are about.

If ever evil thoughts occur to your mind and invade your heart cast them down at the feet of Christ and talk about them frankly to your spiritual father or mother. Take care to avoid any speech that is evil and degenerate. It is also well to avoid empty talk that has no purpose except to raise a laugh. As for laughter that is unrestrained and raucous, it is not good to be attracted to that sort of thing.

---

* See note in Chapter 5.

You should take delight in listening to sacred reading and in often turning generously to prayer. You should also in that prayer daily confess to God with real repentance any evil you have done in the past and for the future have the firm purpose to put right any wrong you may have done.

Don't act out the sensuous desires that occur to you naturally[1] and turn away from the pursuit of your own will. Rather you should follow in obedience the directions your abbot or abbess gives you, even if they, which God forbid, should contradict their own teaching by the way they live. In such a case just remember the Lord's advice about the example of the Pharisees: accept and follow their teaching but on no account imitate their actions.[2]

No one should aspire to gain a reputation for holiness. First of all we must actually become holy; then there would be some truth in having a reputation for it. The way to become holy is faithfully to fulfil God's commandments every day by loving chastity, by hating no one, by avoiding envy and hostile rivalry, by not becoming full of self but showing due respect for our elders and love for those who are younger, by praying in the love of Christ for those who are hostile to us, by seeking reconciliation and peace before the sun goes down whenever we have a quarrel with another,[3] and finally by never despairing of the mercy of God.

These, then, are the guidelines to lead us along the way of spiritual achievement. If we follow them day and night and never on any account give up, so that on judgement day we can give an account of our fidelity to them, that reward will be granted us by the Lord which he himself promised in the scriptures: what no eye has seen nor ear heard God has prepared for those who love him.[4]

The workshop in which we are called to work along these lines with steady perseverance is the enclosure of the monastery and stability in community life.

⁊ℭ

CHAPTER 5

Monastic obedience

THE FIRST STEP ON THE WAY TO HUMILITY IS TO OBEY an order without delaying for a moment. That is a response which comes easily to those who hold nothing dearer than Christ himself. And so, because of the holy service monks and nuns have accepted in their monastic profession or because they fear the self-destruction of hell or value so much the glory of eternal life, as soon as a superior gives them an order it is as though it came from God himself and they cannot endure any delay in carrying out what they have been told to do. Of such servants of his the Lord says that they obeyed him as soon as they heard him.[1] We should remember also that he said to the teachers: whoever listens to you, listens to me.[2]

The obedience of such people leads them to leave aside their own concerns and forsake their own will. They abandon what they have in hand and leave it unfinished. With a ready step inspired by obedience they respond by their action to the voice that summons them. It is, in fact, almost in one single moment that a command is uttered by the superior and the task carried to completion by the disciple, showing how much more quickly both acts are accomplished together because of their reverence for God.

24

Those who are possessed by a real desire to find their way to eternal life don't hesitate to choose the narrow way to which our Lord referred when he said: Narrow is the way that leads to life.[3] They live not to serve their own will nor to give way to their own desires and pleasures, but they submit in their way of life to the decisions and instructions of another, living in a monastery and willingly accepting an abbot or abbess as their superior. No one can doubt that they have as their model that saying of the Lord: I came not to do my own will but the will of him who sent me.[4]

We should remember, however, that such obedience will be acceptable to God and rewarding to us, if we carry out the orders given us in a way that is not fearful, nor slow, nor half-hearted, nor marred by murmuring or the sort of compliance that betrays resentment. Anything like that would be quite wrong because obedience to superiors is obedience to God, as the Lord himself made clear when he said: He who listens to you, listens to me.[5] Indeed, obedience must be given with genuine good will, because God loves a cheerful giver.[6] If obedience is given with a bad will and with murmuring not only in words but even in bitterness of heart, then even though the command may be externally fulfilled it will not be accepted by God, for he can see the resistance in the heart of a murmurer.* One

* Note on 'murmuring' in the Rule. The Latin word 'murmuratio' is vital for St Benedict's teaching on life in community but it defies translation into everyday English. The scriptural source is the murmuring of the Israelites against Moses in the desert (Numbers 14:2). The framework of monastic life is obedience. As presented in Chapter 5 it is more than a juridical concept because external conformity is not enough and inner assent is called for. Other texts in the Rule (especially in the Prologue and Chapter 72) make it clear that the motive of inner assent to obedience must be love – ultimately it is that love of God which Christ proclaimed as mediated through the love of brothers and sisters. In monastic life obedience and love are so intimately bound together that each becomes an expression of the other. Nothing is so corrosive of that ideal as the sort of constant complaining St Benedict has in mind when he writes about 'murmuring' and 'murmurers' in a Benedictine community. The damage is done not by the fact that there is a complaint. There are always procedures for legitimate complaints, which are healthy in a monastic

who behaves in such a way not only fails to receive the reward of grace but actually incurs the punishment deserved by murmurers. Only repentance and reparation can save such a one from this punishment.

⁂

CHAPTER 6

Cherishing silence in the monastery

IN A MONASTERY WE OUGHT TO FOLLOW THE ADVICE of the psalm which says: I have resolved to keep watch over my ways so that I may not sin with my tongue. I am guarded about the way I speak and have accepted silence in humility refraining even from words that are good.[1] In this verse the psalmist shows that, because of the value of silence, there are times when it is best not to speak even though what we have in mind is good. How much more important it is to refrain from evil speech, remembering what such sins bring down on us in punishment. In fact so important is it to cultivate silence, even about matters concerning sacred values and spiritual instruction, that permission to speak should be granted only rarely to monks

---

community provided they are not destructive and are honestly brought forward in a spirit which is open and ready to accept a decision. Murmuring is not like that; it is underhand and quickly becomes part of the 'underlife' of a community. Thus it destroys confidence and is incompatible with the monastic ideals of Chapter 5 and of the Prologue and Chapter 72. In a community it is impossible for the superior to deal with it; it affects others; in the end it affects the spirit of a whole community. For individuals it becomes increasingly addictive and they develop a corresponding blindness to the harm they are doing to themselves and to others. That is the ground for St Benedict's exceptionally severe treatment of it. Murmuring is a technical monastic concept; it is best to retain the word, recognizing its unique meaning.

and nuns although they may themselves have achieved a high standard of monastic observance. After all, it is written in scripture that one who never stops talking cannot avoid falling into sin.[2] Another text in the same book reminds us that the tongue holds the key to death and life.[3] We should remember that speaking and instructing belong to the teacher; the disciple's role is to be silent and listen.

If any, then, have requests to make of the superior they should make them with deference and respect. As for vulgarity and idle gossip repeated for the sake of a laugh, such talk is forbidden at all times and in all places; we should never allow a disciple to utter words like that.

CHAPTER 7

The value of humility

THE WORD OF GOD IN SCRIPTURE TEACHES US IN clear and resounding terms that anyone who lays claim to a high position will be brought low and anyone who is modest in self-appraisal will be lifted up. This is Christ's teaching about the guest who took the first place at the king's banquet: all who exalt themselves, he said, will be humbled and all who humble themselves will be exalted.[1] He taught us by these words that whenever one of us is raised to a position of prominence there is always an element of pride involved. The psalmist shows his concern to avoid this when he says: there is no pride in my heart, O Lord, nor arrogance in the look of my eyes; I have not aspired to a role too great for me nor the glamour of pretensions that are beyond me.[2] We should be wary of such pride. And why does he say this? It is because lack of humility calls for correction and so the psalm goes on: If I failed to keep a modest spirit and raised my ambitions too high, then your correction would come down on me as though I were nothing but a newly weaned child on its mother's lap.[3]

If the peak of our endeavour, then, is to achieve profound humility, if we are eager to be raised to that heavenly height, to which we can climb only through humility during our present life, then let us make for ourselves a ladder like the one which Jacob saw in his dream.[4] On that ladder angels of God were shown to him going up and down in a constant exchange between heaven and earth. It is just such an exchange that we need to establish in our own lives, but with this difference for us: our proud attempts at upward climbing will really bring us down, whereas to step downwards in humility is the way to lift our spirit up towards God.

This ladder, then, will symbolize for each of us our life in this world during which we aspire to be lifted up to heaven by the Lord, if only we can learn humility in our hearts. We can imagine that he has placed the steps of the ladder, held in place by the sides which signify our living body and soul, to invite us to climb on them. Paradoxically, to climb upwards will take us down to earth but stepping down will lift us towards heaven. The steps themselves, then, mark the decisions we are called to make in the exercise of humility and self-discipline.

The first step of humility is to cherish at all times the sense of awe with which we should turn to God. It should drive forgetfulness away; it should keep our minds alive to all God's commandments; it should make us reflect in our hearts again and again that those who despise God and reject his love prepare for themselves that irreversible spiritual death which is meant by hell, just as life in eternity is prepared for those who fear God.

One who follows that way finds protection at all times from sin and vice of thought, of tongue, of hand, of foot, of self-will and of disordered sensual desire, so as to lead a life that is completely open before the scrutiny of God and of his angels who watch over us from hour to hour. This is made clear by the psalmist who shows that God is always present to our very thoughts when he says: God searches the hearts and thoughts of men and women,[5] and again: the Lord knows the thoughts of all,[6] and: from afar you know my thoughts,[7] and again: the thoughts of men and women shall give you praise.[8] Thus it may help one concerned about thoughts that are perverse to repeat the psalmist's heartfelt saying: I shall be blameless in his sight only if I guard myself from my own wickedness.[9]

As to pursuing our own will we are warned against that when scripture says to us: turn away from your own desires;[10] and in the Lord's prayer itself we pray that his will may be brought to fulfilment in us. It will be clear that we have learnt well the lesson against fulfilling our own will if we respond to that warning in scripture: there are ways which seem right to human eyes, but their end plunges down into the depths of hell.[11] Another good sign is to be afraid of what scripture says of those who reject such advice: they are corrupt and have become depraved in their pleasure seeking.[12]

As to sensual desires we should believe that they are not hidden from God, for the psalmist says to the Lord: all my desires are known to you.[13] We must indeed be on our guard against evil desires because spiritual death is not far from the gateway to wrongful pleasure, so that scripture gives us this clear direction: do not pursue your lusts.[14] And so, if the eyes of the Lord are watching the good and the

wicked, and if at all times the Lord looks down from
heaven on the sons and daughters of men to see if any
show understanding in seeking God,[15] and if the angels
assigned to care for us report our deeds to the Lord day
and night, we must be on our guard every hour or else, as
the psalmist says, the time may come when God will
observe us falling into evil and so made worthless. He may
spare us for a while during this life, because he is a loving
father who waits and longs for us to do better, but in the
end his rebuke may come upon us with the words: You
were guilty of these crimes and I was silent.[16]

The second step of humility is not to love having our own
way nor to delight in our own desires. Instead we should
take as our model for imitation the Lord himself when he
says: I have come not to indulge my own desires but to do
the will of him who sent me.[17] Again remember that
scripture says: self-indulgence brings down on us its own
penalty, but there is a crown of victory for submitting to
the demands of others.[18]

The third step of humility is to submit oneself out of love of
God to whatever obedience under a superior may require of
us; it is the example of the Lord himself that we follow in
this way, as we know from St Paul's words: he was made
obedient even unto death.[19]

The fourth step of humility is to go even further than this by
readily accepting in patient and silent endurance, without
thought of giving up or avoiding the issue, any hard and
demanding things that may come our way in the course of
that obedience, even if they include harsh impositions
which are unjust. We are encouraged to such patience by
the words of scripture: whoever perseveres to the very end
will be saved.[20] And again there is the saying of the psalm:
be steadfast in your heart and trust in the Lord.[21] Then
again there is that verse from another psalm: it is for you

we face death all the day long and are counted as sheep for
the slaughter.[22]

Those who follow in that way have a sure hope of reward
from God and they are joyful with St Paul's words on their
lips: in all these things we are more than conquerors
through him who loved us.[23] They remember also the
psalm: you, O God, have tested us and have tried us as
silver is tried; you led us, God, into the snare; you laid a
heavy burden on our backs.[24] Then this is added in the
psalm: you placed leaders over us[25] to show how we should
be under a superior. In this way they fulfil the Lord's
command through patience in spite of adversity and in spite
of any wrongs they may suffer; struck on one cheek they
offer the other; when robbed of their coat they let their
cloak go also; pressed to go one mile they willingly go
two;[26] with the Apostle Paul they put up with false brethren
and shower blessings on those who curse them.[27]

The fifth step of humility is that we should not cover up but
humbly confess to our superior or spiritual guide whatever
evil thoughts come into our minds and the evil deeds we
have done in secret. That is what scripture urges on us
when it says: make known to the Lord the way you have
taken and trust in him.[28] Then again it says: confess to the
Lord, for he is good, for his mercy endures for ever.[29] And
again: I have made known to you my sin and have not
covered over my wrongdoing. I have said: against myself I
shall proclaim my own faults to the Lord and you have
forgiven the wickedness of my heart.[30]

The sixth step of humility for monks or nuns is to accept
without complaint really wretched and inadequate
conditions so that when faced with a task of any kind
they would think of themselves as poor workers not
worthy of consideration and repeat to God the verse of the
psalm: I am of no account and lack understanding, no

better than a beast in your sight. Yet I am always in your presence.[31]

The seventh step of humility is that we should be ready to speak of ourselves as of less importance and less worthy than others, not as a mere phrase on our lips but we should really believe it in our hearts. Thus in a spirit of humility we make the psalmist's words our own: I am no more than a worm with no claim to be a human person for I am despised by others and cast out by my own people.[32] I was raised up high in honour, but then I was humbled and overwhelmed with confusion.[33] In the end we may learn to say: it was good for me, Lord, that you humbled me so that I might learn your precepts.[34]

The eighth step of humility teaches us to do nothing which goes beyond what is approved and encouraged by the common rule of the monastery and the example of our seniors.

The ninth step of humility leads us to refrain from unnecessary speech and to guard our silence by not speaking until we are addressed. That is what scripture recommends with these sayings: anyone who is forever chattering will not escape sin[35] and there is another saying from a psalm: one who never stops talking loses the right way in life.[36]

The tenth step of humility teaches that we should not be given to empty laughter on every least occasion because: a fool's voice is for ever raised in laughter.[37]

The eleventh step of humility is concerned with the manner of speech appropriate in a monastery. We should speak gently and seriously with words that are weighty and restrained. We should be brief and reasonable in whatever we have to say and not raise our voices to insist on our own opinions.

The wise, we should remember, are to be recognized in words that are few.

The twelfth step of humility is concerned with the external impression conveyed by those dedicated to monastic life. The humility of their hearts should be apparent by their bodily movements to all who see them. Whether they are at the work of God, at prayer in the oratory, walking about the monastery, in the garden, on a journey or in the fields, wherever they may be, whether sitting, walking or standing they should be free of any hint of arrogance or pride in their manner or the way they look about them. They should guard their eyes and look down. They should remember their sins and their guilt before the judgement of God, with the words of the publican in the gospel for ever on their lips as he stood with his eyes cast down saying: Lord, I am not worthy, sinner that I am, to lift my eyes to the heavens.[38] Or the words of the psalmist might fit just as well: I am bowed down and utterly humbled.[39]

Any monk or nun who has climbed all these steps of humility will come quickly to that love of God which in its fullness casts out all fear. Carried forward by that love, such a one will begin to observe without effort as though they were natural all those precepts which in earlier days were kept at least partly through fear. A new motive will have taken over, not fear of hell but the love of Christ. Good habit and delight in virtue will carry us along. This happy state the Lord will bring about through the Holy Spirit in his servant whom he has cleansed of vice and sin and taught to be a true and faithful worker in the Kingdom.

❧

CHAPTER 8

The Divine Office at night

IT SEEMS REASONABLE THAT DURING WINTERTIME, that is from the first of November until Easter all should arise at the eighth hour of the night. By that time, having rested until a little after midnight, they may rise with their food well digested. Any time which is left after Vigils should be devoted to study of the psalter or lessons by those who are behind hand in these tasks. From Easter until the first of November the times should be arranged so that there is a very short break after Vigils for the needs of nature. Lauds can then follow at the first light of daybreak.

CHAPTER 9

The number of psalms at the night office

DURING THIS WINTER SEASON THE OFFICE OF VIGILS begins with this verse recited three times; Lord, open my lips and my mouth will declare your praise.[1] To this should be added the third psalm and the *Gloria*. Then will come the ninety fourth psalm chanted with its antiphon and after that an Ambrosian hymn, followed by six psalms with their antiphons.

On the completion of these psalms there is a versicle and a blessing from the abbot or abbess. Then all sit on benches while three lessons are read out from the lectern by members of the choir, taking it in turns. Responsories are sung after each but the *Gloria Patri* comes only after the third and as soon as the cantor intones it all rise from their seats out of reverence for the Holy Trinity. The readings at Vigils are to be taken from the inspired books of the Old and New Testaments with commentaries on them by recognized and orthodox catholic Fathers.

After these three lessons with their responsories there follow six psalms which are to be sung with the *alleluia*. A reading from the Apostle recited by heart should follow with a verse and the petition from the litany, that is: Lord, have mercy. That brings the night Vigils to a conclusion.

CHAPTER 10

The night office in summertime

FROM EASTER UNTIL THE FIRST DAY OF NOVEMBER the same number of psalms should be said as we have established for winter, but because the nights are shorter, instead of reading three lessons from the book on the lectern only one should be recited by heart from the Old Testament with a brief responsory to follow. Apart from that the arrangements for winter are followed exactly so that never less than twelve psalms should be recited at Vigils, not counting the third and ninety fourth psalms.

CHAPTER 11

Vigils or night office on Sunday

ALL SHOULD RISE EARLIER FOR THE NIGHT-TIME
vigils on Sunday. In these Vigils the arrangement should be
that six psalms and a verse should be chanted, as described
above, and then, when everyone has sat down in an orderly
way on the benches, four lessons should be read from the
book on the lectern with their responsories. The *Gloria* is
added only to the fourth lesson and when the cantor begins to
sing it, all rise out of reverence. The other six psalms follow
these lessons in due order with their responsories and a
versicle, as described above. After that, four more lessons
should be read in the same way with their responsories. Then
three canticles from the prophets, chosen by the superior, are
chanted with the *alleluia*. Then after a versicle and blessing
from the abbot or abbess, four further lessons should be read
from the New Testament, as described above. After the
fourth, the superior intones the *Te Deum laudamus* and at
the end of that reads the gospel while all in the choir stand as
a sign of profound reverence. At the end of the gospel all
respond with *Amen* and the superior intones the *Te decet laus*
and after the blessing Lauds begins.

This arrangement for Vigils is followed in the same way on
every Sunday both in summer and winter, unless – which
God forbid – the community gets up late, in which case the
lessons or responsories should to some extent be shortened.
Care, however, should be taken to avoid this. If it should
happen, whoever is responsible must express fitting
repentance to God in the oratory.

CHAPTER 12

The celebration of solemn Lauds

FOR LAUDS ON SUNDAY THE SIXTY SIXTH PSALM
should be said first of all straight through without an
antiphon. After that comes the fiftieth psalm with its
alleluia. Then come the hundred and seventeenth psalm and
the sixty second followed by the *Benedicite* and *Laudate*
psalms, a reading from the book of the Apocalypse recited
by heart, the responsory, an Ambrosian hymn, a versicle,
the *Benedictus*, litany and conclusion.

❦

CHAPTER 13

Lauds on ordinary days

ON ORDINARY DAYS LAUDS SHOULD BE CELEBRATED
like this: the sixty sixth psalm should be said with its
antiphon but rather slowly, as on Sunday, to make sure
that all are present for the fiftieth psalm which is said
with its antiphon. Two other psalms are said after that
according to the usual arrangement, namely: on Monday
the fifth and thirty fifth; on Tuesday the forty second and
fifty sixth; on Wednesday the sixty third and sixty fourth;
on Thursday the eighty seventh and eighty ninth; on Friday
the seventy fifth and ninety first; on Saturday the one
hundred and forty second and the canticle from
Deuteronomy divided into two sections with the *Gloria*
following each section. On the other days a canticle is

recited from the prophets on the days allotted by the Roman Church. Then come the *Laudate* psalms of praise, a reading from the apostle recited by heart, a responsory, an Ambrosian hymn, a versicle, the *Benedictus*, the litany and the conclusion.

It is important that the celebration of Lauds and Vespers should never be concluded without the recitation by the superior of the whole of the Lord's prayer so that all may hear and attend to it. This is because of the harm that is often done in a community by the thorns of conflict which can arise. Bound by the very words of that prayer 'forgive us as we also forgive' they will be cleansed from the stain of such evil. At the other offices only the ending of the Lord's prayer is said aloud so that all may respond: 'but deliver us from evil'.[1]

⁂

CHAPTER 14

The celebration of Vigils on feasts of saints

ON THE FEASTS OF SAINTS AND ON ALL OTHER solemnities Vigils should follow the order laid down for the celebration of Sunday except that the psalms, antiphons and readings that are appropriate to the day should be recited; the order of the liturgy itself remains the same as that described for Sunday.

⁂

CHAPTER 15

When the Alleluia should be said

FROM THE HOLY FEAST OF EASTER UNTIL PENTECOST the *Alleluia* must always be said in the psalms and the responsories. From Pentecost until the beginning of Lent it is said only with the last six psalms in the night office. On every Sunday outside Lent, however, the *alleluia* is included in Lauds, Prime, Terce, Sext and None, but at Vespers an antiphon is intoned instead. The *alleluia* is never added to the responsories except from Easter to Pentecost.

CHAPTER 16

The hours of the work of God during the day

THE WORDS OF THE PSALM ARE: I HAVE UTTERED your praises seven times during the day.[1] We shall fulfil that sacred number of seven if at the times of Lauds, Prime, Terce, Sext, None, Vespers and Compline we perform the duty of our service to God, because it was of these day hours that the psalm said: I have uttered your praise seven times during the day. About the night Vigil that same psalm says: In the middle of the night I arose to praise you.[2] And so at these times let us offer praise to our Creator because of his justice revealed in his judgements[3] – that is at Lauds, Prime, Terce, Sext, None, Vespers and Compline and in the night let us arise to praise him.

CHAPTER 17

The number of psalms to be sung at the hours

WE HAVE ALREADY SET OUT THE ORDER OF THE
psalms for Vigils and for Lauds. Now let us look at the
order of the psalms for the rest of the Hours. At Prime
three psalms should be recited separately and not under one
Gloria and a hymn appropriate to each hour should be said
after the *Deus in adiutorium* before the psalms are begun.
After the three psalms there should be one lesson and the
Hour is concluded with a versicle and 'Lord have mercy'
and the concluding prayers.

At Terce, Sext and None the same order of prayer obtains,
that is, after the opening verse and the hymn for each Hour
there are three psalms, a reading, versicle, 'Lord have
mercy' and the conclusion. If the community is a large one
they have antiphons as well but, if it is small, they sing the
psalms alone.

For the office of Vespers the number of psalms should be
limited to four with their antiphons. After the psalms a
lesson is repeated, then a responsory, an Ambrosian hymn,
a versicle, the *Magnificat*, litany and the Hour is concluded
with the Lord's prayer.

Compline will consist in the recitation of three psalms on
their own without antiphons. Then comes the hymn for
Compline, one lesson, a versicle, 'Lord have mercy' and the
Office is concluded with a blessing.

CHAPTER 18

The order for reciting the psalms

EACH HOUR BEGINS WITH THE FOLLOWING VERSE: O
God come to my assistance, O Lord make haste to help me.
The *Gloria* and the hymn for each Hour then follow.

At Prime on Sunday four sections of psalm one hundred and
eighteen are said and at the other Hours, that is at Terce,
Sext and None, three sections of the same psalm are said.
At Prime on Monday there are three psalms, namely the
first, second and sixth and so on for each day at Prime
until Sunday when three psalms are said in order up to the
nineteenth psalm, but the ninth and seventeenth are divided
into two. This will mean that Vigils on Sunday always
begin with the twentieth psalm.

Then at Terce, Sext and None on Monday the nine sections
left over from the one hundred and eighteenth psalm are
recited – three at each of these hours. That psalm is
completed, then, in two days, namely Sunday and Monday,
and on Tuesday at Terce, Sext and None three psalms are
sung at each Hour starting from the one hundred and
nineteenth and going on to the one hundred and twenty
seventh, that is nine psalms. These same psalms are
repeated daily until Sunday and the identical arrangement
of hymns, lessons and verses is retained every day. That
means, of course, that the series always starts again on
Sunday with the one hundred and eighteenth psalm.

Vespers each day has four psalms to be sung. These psalms
should start with the one hundred and ninth going through
to the one hundred and forty seventh, omitting those which
are taken from that series for other Hours, that is the one

hundred and seventeenth to the one hundred and twenty
seventh and the one hundred and thirty third and the one
hundred and forty second; with these exceptions all the
others are sung at Vespers. But since that leaves us short
of three psalms the longer psalms in this series should be
divided in two, that is the one hundred and thirty eighth,
the one hundred and forty third and the one hundred and
forty fourth. The one hundred and sixteenth psalm,
however, because it is very short should be joined to the
one hundred and fifteenth. With the order of psalmody
thus arranged for Vespers the rest of the office, that is the
lesson, response, hymn, versicle and *Magnificat* should
follow the principles which are set out above. At Compline
the same psalms are recited daily, that is the fourth,
ninetieth and one hundred and thirty third.

After we have arranged the psalms for the day Hours in this
way all the other psalms which are left over should be
divided equally between the Vigils on the seven nights of
the week, which can be done by dividing the longer psalms
and allotting twelve psalms or divisions to each night.

We have no hesitation in urging that, if any are dissatisfied
with this distribution of psalms they should re-arrange them
in whatever way seems better, provided that one principle
is preserved, namely that the whole psalter of one hundred
and fifty psalms should be recited each week and that the
series should start again on Sunday at Vigils. Any monastic
community which chants less than the full psalter with the
usual canticles each week shows clearly that it is too
indolent in the devotion of its service of God. After all, we
read that our holy Fathers had the energy to fulfil in one
single day what we in our lukewarm devotion only aspire
to complete in a whole week.

CHAPTER 19

Our approach to prayer

GOD IS PRESENT EVERYWHERE – PRESENT TO THE
good and to the evil as well, so that nothing anyone does
escapes his notice; that is the firm conviction of our faith.
Let us be very sure, however, without a moment's doubt
that his presence to us is never so strong as while we are
celebrating the work of God in the oratory. And so we
should always recall at such times the words of the psalm:
serve the Lord with awe and reverence,[1] and: sing the
Lord's praises with skill and relish,[2] and: I shall sing your
praise in the presence of the angels.[3] All of us, then, should
reflect seriously on how to appear before the majesty of
God in the presence of his angels. That will lead us to
make sure that, when we sing in choir, there is complete
harmony between the thoughts in our mind and the
meaning of the words we sing.

※

CHAPTER 20

The ideal of true reverence in prayer

IF IN ORDINARY LIFE WE HAVE A FAVOUR TO ASK OF
someone who has power and authority, we naturally
approach that person with due deference and respect. When
we come, then, with our requests in prayer before the Lord,
who is God of all creation, is it not all the more important
that we should approach him in a spirit of real humility

and a devotion that is open to him alone and free from distracting thoughts? We really must be quite clear that our prayer will be heard, not because of the eloquence and length of all we have to say, but because of the heartfelt repentance and openness of our hearts to the Lord whom we approach. Our prayer should, therefore, be free from all other preoccupations and it should normally be short, although we may well on occasions be inspired to stay longer in prayer through the gift of God's grace working within us. Our prayer together in community, on the other hand, should always be moderate in length and when the sign is given by the superior all should rise together.

⚜

CHAPTER 21

The deans of the monastery

DEANS SHOULD BE CHOSEN FROM AMONG THE community, if that is justified by its size. They should be chosen for their good reputation and high monastic standards of life. Their office will be to take care of all the needs of the groups of ten placed under them and to do so in all respects in accordance with God's commandments and the instructions of their superior. They must be selected for their suitability in character and gifts so that the abbot or abbess may, without anxiety, share some responsibilities with them. For that reason they should not be chosen simply because of their order in the community but because of their upright lives and the wisdom of their teaching.

If any of the deans are affected by some breath of pride which lays them open to adverse criticism, they should be corrected once or twice or even three times. After that, if any are unwilling to change for the better, they should be deposed from their position of responsibility so that another who is more worthy of the office may be brought in. In the case of the prior or prioress we propose the same course of action.

※

CHAPTER 22

Sleeping arrangements for the community

THE MEMBERS OF THE COMMUNITY SHOULD EACH have beds for themselves and they should all receive from the superior bedding which is suitable to monastic life. If possible they should all sleep in one room, but if the community is too large for that they should sleep in groups of ten or twenty with senior members among them to care for them. A lamp should be kept alight in the dormitories until the morning.

They should sleep in their normal clothes wearing a belt or cord round their waists; but they should not keep knives in their belts for fear of cutting themselves accidentally while asleep. All should be prepared to rise immediately without any delay as soon as the signal to get up is given; then they should hurry to see who can get first to the oratory for the work of God, but of course they should do this with due dignity and restraint. The young should not have their beds next to each other but they should be placed among those of the seniors. In the morning, as they are getting up for the work of God, they should quietly give encouragement to those who are sleepy and given to making excuses for being late.

❧

CHAPTER 23

Faults which deserve excommunication

IF AN INDIVIDUAL IN THE COMMUNITY IS DEFIANT, disobedient, proud or given to murmuring or in any other way set in opposition to the holy Rule and contemptuous of traditions of the seniors, then we should follow the precept of our Lord. Such a one should be warned once and then twice in private by seniors. If there is no improvement, the warning should be followed by a severe public rebuke before the whole community. If even this does not bring reform then excommunication should be the next penalty, provided that the meaning of such a punishment is really understood. In a case of real defiance, corporal punishment may be the only cure.

❧

CHAPTER 24

Different degrees of severity in punishment

THE SEVERITY OF EXCOMMUNICATION OR ANY OTHER punishment should correspond to the gravity of the fault committed, and it is for the superior to decide about the seriousness of faults. Anyone found guilty of faults which are not too serious should be excluded from taking part in community meals at the common table. This exclusion from the common table also means that in the oratory the guilty person will not be allowed to lead a psalm or antiphon nor to recite a reading until satisfaction has been made. Meals should be provided for such a one to take alone after the community meal at, for instance, the ninth hour, if the community eats at the sixth or after Vespers, if the community eats at the ninth hour. That regime should continue until fitting satisfaction has been made and pardon granted.

CHAPTER 25

Punishment for more serious faults

ANYONE WITH THE INFECTION OF A REALLY SERIOUS offence is to be excluded not only from the common table but from common prayer in the oratory as well. None of the community should associate with or talk to the guilty person, who is to persevere alone in sorrow and penance in whatever work has been allotted, remembering St Paul's fearful judgement when he wrote to the Corinthians that: such a one should be handed over for the destruction of the flesh so that the spirit may be saved on the day of the Lord.[1] As for meals, they are to be provided in solitude and the abbot or abbess must decide the amounts and the times that are appropriate. No one should offer a blessing in passing the guilty person nor should the food provided be blessed.

CHAPTER 26

Unlawful association with the excommunicated

IF ANY MEMBER OF THE COMMUNITY PRESUMES
without the permission of the abbot or abbess to associate
in any way with or speak to or give instructions to one
who has been excommunicated then that person should
receive exactly the same punishment of excommunication.

৵

CHAPTER 27

The superior's care for the excommunicated

EVERY POSSIBLE CARE AND CONCERN SHOULD BE
shown for those who have been excommunicated by the
abbot or abbess, who are themselves also to remember that
it is not the healthy who need a physician but the sick.[1]
Therefore the superior should use every curative skill as a
wise doctor does, for instance by sending in *senpectae*, that
is, mature and wise senior members of the community who
may discreetly bring counsel to one who is in a state of
uncertainty and confusion; their task will be to show the
sinner the way to humble reconciliation and also to bring
consolation, as St Paul also urges,[2] to one in danger of
being overwhelmed by excessive sorrow and in need of the
reaffirmation of love which everyone in the community
must achieve through their prayer.

As for the abbot or abbess, they must show the greatest possible concern with great wisdom and perseverance to avoid losing any one of the sheep committed to their care. They should be well aware that they have undertaken an office which is more like the care of the sick than the exercise of power over the healthy. They should be anxious to avoid the Lord's rebuke to the shepherds through the Prophet Ezekiel: you made your own those you saw to be fat and healthy and cast out those who were weak.[3] They should follow the loving example of the Good Shepherd who left ninety-nine of his flock on the mountains and went off to look for the one sheep who had strayed. So great was his compassion for the weakness of that one erring sheep that he actually lifted it onto his sacred shoulders and so carried it back to the rest of the flock.

CHAPTER 28

The treatment of those who relapse

IF THERE SHOULD BE ANY WHO HAVE BEEN frequently reproved for some fault and have not reformed, even after excommunication, there is a sharper correction to be applied; that is to subject such a one to the punishment of the rod. But if even this does not bring reform and if – may God forbid it – the guilty one is puffed up with pride to the point of wanting to defend wrongful actions, then the superior must follow the practice of an experienced doctor. After applying dressings and the ointment of exhortation and the medicine of divine scripture and proceeding to the extreme resource of cauterization by excommunication and strokes of the rod,

and if even then the superior sees that no such efforts are
of any avail, yet another remedy must be brought to bear
which is still more powerful, namely the personal prayer
of the superior and of all the community that the Lord,
who can do all things, may himself bring healing to the
delinquent. If even such prayer does not bring healing, the
superior must turn to the knife of amputation, following
the guidance of St Paul, who told the Corinthians to banish
the evil from their midst,[1] and again he said: if the
unfaithful one wishes to go, let him go, lest one diseased
sheep corrupt the whole flock.[2]

⚜

CHAPTER 29

The readmission of any who leave the monastery

ANYONE WHO IS GUILTY OF SERIOUS WRONG BY THE
personal decision to leave the monastery but then asks to
be received back again must first of all promise full
reparation for leaving the monastery. That will be enough
for restoration into the community, but it must be in the
lowest place as a test of humility. If the same monk or nun
departs again, they may be received back until the third
time, but after that all must understand that any question
of return to the community is to be refused.

⚜

CHAPTER 30

The correction of young children

THERE IS A PROPER WAY OF DEALING WITH EVERY age and every degree of understanding, and we should find the right way of dealing with the young. Thus children and adolescents or others who are unable to appreciate the seriousness of excommunication need some other mode of correction, when they go astray. If they are guilty of bad behaviour, then they should be subjected to severe fasting or sharp strokes of the rod to bring them to a better disposition.

❧

CHAPTER 31

The qualities required by the cellarer

THE CELLARER OF THE MONASTERY SHOULD BE chosen from among the community. To qualify for this choice a candidate should be wise and mature in behaviour, sober and not an excessive eater, not proud nor apt to give offence nor inclined to cause trouble, not unpunctual, nor wasteful but living in the fear of God and ready to show the community all the love a father or mother would show to their family. The cellarer will be responsible for the care of all the monastery's goods but must do nothing without the authority of the superior, being content to look after what is committed to the cellarer's care without causing annoyance to the community. If one of the community comes with an unreasonable request, the cellarer should, in refusing what is asked, be careful not to give the impression of personal rejection and so hurt the petitioner's feelings. Such a refusal of an ill-judged request should be measured and given with due deference towards the person involved. As an incentive to personal spiritual progress the cellarer might remember St Paul's saying that those who give good service to others earn a good reputation.[1] The cellarer should show special concern and practical care for the sick and the young, for guests and for the poor, and never forget the account to be rendered for all these responsibilities on the day of judgement. All the utensils of the monastery and in fact everything that belongs to the monastery should be cared for as though they were the sacred vessels of the altar. There must be no negligence on the part of the cellarer nor any tendency to avarice nor to prodigality nor extravagance with the goods of the monastery. The administration should be carried out in all respects with moderation and in accordance with the instructions of the abbot or abbess.

Among the most important qualities the cellarer needs to cultivate is humility and the ability to give a pleasant answer even when a request must be refused. Remember how scripture says that a kindly word is of greater value than a gift, however precious.[2] Although the cellarer's responsibility embraces all that is delegated by the superior there must be no attempt to include what the superior has forbidden. The community should receive their allotted food without any self-important fuss or delay on the part of the cellarer which might provoke them to resentment. The cellarer should remember what is deserved, according to the Lord's saying, by those who provoke to sin one of his little ones.[3]

If the community is large, the cellarer must receive the assistance of helpers whose support will make the burden of this office tolerable. There will, of course, be appropriate times for the cellarer to hand out what is needed and for requests for goods or services to be made; these times should be observed by all so that failure to respect them may not cause any disturbance or unhappiness in the house of God.

CHAPTER 32

The tools and property of the monastery

THE SUPERIOR SHOULD ENTRUST THE PROPERTY OF the monastery consisting in tools, clothing or any other items to various members of the community whose character and reliability inspire confidence. Their job will be to take care of the various articles, assigned to their care individually, and to issue them for use and collect them again afterwards. The superior should keep a list with the details of what has been issued to them so that, when one member of the community succeeds another in any responsibility, there may be no doubt about what items have been entrusted to each individual and what they have returned at the end.

Anyone who is negligent in dealing with the monastery property or allows it to deteriorate must be corrected with a view to improvement. If there is no improvement the one responsible should be subjected to the appropriate discipline of the Rule.

CHAPTER 33

Personal possessions in the monastery

IT IS VITALLY IMPORTANT TO CUT OUT BY THE ROOTS
from the monastery the bad practice of anyone in the
community giving away anything or accepting any gift for
themselves, as though it were their own personal property,
without the permission of the superior. Those in monastic
vows should not claim any property as their own exclusive
possession – absolutely nothing at all, not even books and
writing materials. After all they cannot count even their
bodies and their wills as their own, consecrated, as they
are, to the Lord. They may expect that everything they
need in their lives will be supplied by the superior of the
community without whose permission they may not retain
for themselves anything at all. Following the practice of the
early church described in Acts, everything in the monastery
should be held in common and no one should think of
claiming personal ownership of anything.[1] If any in the
community are found to be addicted to this wicked
practice, they must be warned on the first and second
occasion and then, if there is no improvement, subjected
to punishment.

CHAPTER 34

Fair provision for the needs of all

THIS PRINCIPLE FROM SCRIPTURE SHOULD BE established in the monastery, namely that distribution was made to each in accordance with their needs.[1] This, however, should not be taken to mean that favouritism of individuals can be tolerated; far from it. It should simply be a way of showing proper consideration for needs arising from individual weakness. Those who do not need as much as some others should thank God for the strength they have been given and not be sorry for themselves. Those who need more should be humble about their weakness and not become self-important in enjoying the indulgence granted them. In that way all in the community will be at peace with each other. Above all the evil of murmuring* must not for any reason at all be shown by any word or gesture. Anyone found indulging in such a fault must be subjected to really severe discipline.

CHAPTER 35

Weekly servers in the kitchen and at table

EVERYONE IN THE COMMUNITY SHOULD TAKE TURNS serving in the kitchen and at table. None should be exonerated from kitchen duty except in the case of sickness

---

* See note in Chapter 5.

or the call of some important business for the monastery, because serving each other in this way has the great merit of fostering charity. Nevertheless those who are not very strong should be given assistance to make sure that they will not be distressed by the demands of this work. In fact all should receive the assistance they need because of the regime under which they may be living and the conditions of the locality. In a large community the cellarer should be excused from kitchen service and that should apply also, as we have said, to those engaged in the more demanding business of the monastery. All others in the community must take their turn in serving in a spirit of charity.

On Saturday those who have completed their service should do the washing. This should include the towels which are used by the community when they wash their hands and feet. The feet of all should be washed by the one beginning a week of service as well as the one completing it. All the vessels used in their service should be returned to the cellarer in a clean and sound condition. The cellarer can then pass them on to those taking up these duties with a reliable record of what has been returned and what has been issued again.

One hour before the time of a meal those serving in the kitchen and at table should each receive a drink and some bread in addition to their regular portion. This will help them to serve the community at mealtime without stress and without murmuring* about their lot. On days, however, when there is the solemn celebration of a feast they should wait until after Mass.

On Sundays after the celebration of Lauds the weekly servers should bow low before all the community asking for their prayers. The server who has completed a week intones

---

* See note in Chapter 5.

three times the verse: 'Blessed are you, Lord God, because you have helped me and given me consolation'[1] and then receives a blessing. The one beginning the week follows on three times with the verse: 'O God, come to my assistance, Lord, make haste to help me'[2] and after the verse has been repeated by everyone receives a blessing and begins a week of service.

⚜

CHAPTER 36

The care of the sick in the monastery

THE CARE OF THOSE WHO ARE SICK IN THE community is an absolute priority, which must rank before every other requirement, so that there may be no doubt that it is Christ who is truly served in them. After all Christ himself said: I was sick and you came to visit me, and also: what you did to one of these my least brethren you did to me.[1] The sick themselves, on the other hand, should reflect that the care and attention they receive is offered them to show honour to God and so they must be careful not to distress by selfish and unreasonable demands those attending to their needs. Still such behaviour in the sick should be tolerated by those attending them, who will receive a richer reward for such patience. The abbot or abbess should certainly make very sure that the sick suffer no neglect.

Separate infirmary accommodation should be provided for the sick with a member of the community in charge who has true reverence for God and can be relied on to meet the needs of the patients with sensitive care. The sick may be offered baths whenever it will help, although those in good health and especially the young should not be given this permission so easily. The sick who are really failing may be allowed to eat meat to restore their strength, but when they get better they should all abstain from meat as usual.

The abbot or abbess should keep a careful eye on the sick to make sure that they suffer no neglect through the forgetfulness of the cellarer or infirmary staff, because the responsibility for the shortcomings of their disciples rests on them.

CHAPTER 37

Care for the elderly and the young

HUMAN NATURE ITSELF IS DRAWN TO TENDER concern for those in the two extremes of age and youth, but the authority of the Rule should reinforce this natural instinct. Their frailty should always be given consideration so that they should not be strictly bound to the provisions of the Rule in matters of diet. They should receive loving consideration and be allowed to anticipate the regular hours laid down for food and drink.

CHAPTER 38

The weekly reader

THERE SHOULD ALWAYS BE READING FOR THE community during meal times. The reader, however, should not be one who has taken up the book casually to read without preparation, but whoever reads should do so for a whole week beginning on Sunday. Then after Mass and Communion the reader should ask for the assistance of the prayers of all the community to ward off the spirit of pride in the performance of this task. So before God in the oratory this verse should be intoned three times by all after the incoming reader has begun the chant: 'O Lord, open my lips and my mouth shall proclaim your praise'.[1] With the blessing that will follow the reader can safely begin the week of reading in public.

During meals there should be complete silence disturbed by no whispering nor should anyone's voice be heard except the reader's. Everyone in the community should be attentive to the needs of their neighbours as they eat and drink so that there should be no need for anyone to ask for what they require. However, if such a need should arise there should be agreed signs for such requests so as to avoid the sound of voices. No one should venture to ask a question about the reading during meal times nor about anything else for fear of giving opportunities which would destroy the spirit of silence. The only exception is that the superior might wish to make some comment for the instruction of all.

The weekly reader can eat afterwards with the cooks and servers for the week but should also be given a drink of watered wine just before starting to read because of Holy

Communion and also to relieve the burden of a long fast.
The choice of readers should be determined by their ability
to read intelligibly to others and not by their order in the
community.

⁂

CHAPTER 39

The amount of food to be made available

WHETHER THE MAIN MEAL EACH DAY IS AT NOON OR
in mid-afternoon, two cooked dishes on every table should
be enough to allow for differences of taste so that those
who feel unable to eat from one may be satisfied with the
other. Two dishes, then, should be enough for the needs of
all, but if there is a supply of fruit and fresh vegetables
available a third may be added. A full pound of bread
every day for each member of the community should be
enough both on days when there is only one meal and on
those when there is a supper as well as dinner. If the
community is to have supper the cellarer must retain a
third of each one's bread ration to give them at supper.

If, however, the workload of the community is especially
heavy it will be for the abbot or abbess at the time to
decide whether it is right to make some addition to the
amount of food made available. We must always be careful,
however, to avoid excessive eating which might also cause
indigestion. Nothing is so opposed to Christian values as
overeating, as we can see from the words of our Lord:
take care that your hearts are not weighed down by
overeating.[1]

The same quantities should not be served to young children as to adults. They should receive less which will preserve in this, as in all monastic practice, the principle of frugality. Everyone should abstain completely from eating the flesh of four-footed animals except, of course, the sick whose strength needs building up.

❧

CHAPTER 40

The proper amount of drink to be provided

ST PAUL SAYS THAT EACH OF US HAS A SPECIAL GIFT from God, one kind for one of us and quite a different one for another.[1] That reflection makes me reluctant to decide on the measure of food and drink for others. However, having due regard for the weakness of those whose health is not robust, perhaps a half-measure of wine every day should suffice for each member of the community. As for those to whom God has given the self-control that enables them to abstain from strong drink, they should be encouraged by the knowledge that the Lord will also give them a fitting reward.

Of course, the local conditions or the nature of the community's work or the heat of summer may suggest that a more liberal allowance of drink is needed by the community. In that case it lies with the superior to decide what is needed to meet these conditions while at the same time guarding against the subtle danger of excessive drinking leading to drunkenness. We do, indeed, read that wine is entirely unsuitable as a drink for monks and nuns but, since in our day they cannot all be brought to accept

this, let us at least agree that we should drink in
moderation and not till we are full. The words of scripture
should warn us: wine makes even the wise turn away from
the truth.[2]

It may be that local circumstances may make it impossible to
provide the amount of wine we have suggested above so
that there may be much less available or even none at all.
Those who live in such a locality should praise God and
avoid any murmuring.* Above all else I urge that there
should be no murmuring in the community.

⚜

CHAPTER 41

The times for community meals

FROM EASTER TO PENTECOST THE COMMUNITY
should have dinner at noon and supper in the evening. From
Pentecost throughout the whole summer on Wednesday and
Friday they should normally fast until mid-afternoon,
provided that they are not working out in the fields or
exposed to an excessively hot summer. On other days dinner
should be at noon, but it is for the superior to decide whether
noon should be the time for dinner every day, if they have
work to do in the fields and the summer heat is too much. The
principle is that the superior should manage everything so
prudently that the saving work of grace may be accomplished
in the community and whatever duties the community
undertakes they may be carried out without any excuse for
murmuring.

* See note in Chapter 5.

From the thirteenth of September until the beginning of Lent dinner will always be in mid-afternoon. Then from the beginning of Lent until Easter they eat after Vespers which should be timed so that lamps are not needed during the meal and everything can be completed by the light of day. That should always be the principle to determine the time of supper or the fast-day meal, namely that all should be done while it is still light.

※

CHAPTER 42

The great silence after Compline

SILENCE SHOULD BE SOUGHT AT ALL TIMES BY MONKS and nuns and this is especially important for them at night time. The final community act, then, before the great silence throughout the year both on fast days and on ordinary days should be the same. On ordinary days as soon as the community rises from supper they should go and sit down together while one of them reads from the Conferences of Cassian or the Lives of the Fathers or from some other text which will be inspiring at that time. However, the Heptateuch or the Book of Kings should not be chosen because these texts might prove disturbing to those of rather delicate feelings so late in the evening; they should be read at other times.

On fast days there should be a short interval after Vespers and then all should assemble for the reading of the *Conferences* as we have already described. Four or five pages should be read or as many as time permits so that everyone can gather together during this period of reading in case anyone has been assigned to a task and is detained by it. As soon as everyone is present they celebrate Compline together. It is after that, when they leave the oratory at the end of Compline, that there must be no further permission for anyone to speak at all. Any infringement of this rule of silence which comes to light must incur severe punishment. There may be an exception if some need of the guests requires attention or if the superior has occasion to give someone an order. If something like that cannot be avoided, it should be performed with great tact and the restraint which good manners require.

CHAPTER 43

Late-comers for the work of God or in the refectory

WHEN THE TIME COMES FOR ONE OF THE DIVINE offices to begin, as soon as the signal is heard, everyone must set aside whatever they may have in hand and hurry as fast as possible to the oratory, but of course they should do so in a dignified way which avoids giving rise to any boisterous behaviour. The essential point is that nothing should be accounted more important than the work of God.

Vigils start with Psalm 94 and we want this to be recited at a slow and meditative pace to give time for all to gather. Then, if anyone arrives after the *Gloria* of that psalm, they may not join the choir in their proper order but must take a place apart, which the superior has established at the end of the choir order for any who fail in this way. That will mean that as offenders they will be in full view of the superior and all the community until they purge their offence by public penance at the end of the office. The reason for deciding that they should stand in the last place and apart from everyone else is so that shame itself may teach them to do better. If they were excluded and made to stay outside the oratory, there might be some who would actually go back to bed for further sleep, or they might sit outside and gossip with each other so that an opportunity would be given to the devil to lead them astray. They should go inside just as I have described which will bring them to better standards and not abandon them to the worst consequences of their fault.

During the day hours any who arrive at the work of God after the introduction and the *Gloria* of the first psalm which follows it must stand in the last place, as explained above. They must not presume to join the rest of the choir without doing penance, unless the superior permits it as an exception; even in that case the one who is at fault should apologize.

In the refectory all must come to table together so as to offer their grace together as one community. Any, therefore, who through carelessness or some other personal fault do not arrive in the refectory in time for grace should simply be corrected until after the second occurrence of this failure. If there is no improvement after that they should not be allowed a place at the common table but should eat separately out of contact with the rest of the community and be deprived of their portion of wine until they have made due apology and reformed their behaviour. Anyone failing to be present at grace after meals should be treated in the same way.

None may take it on themselves to eat or drink before or
after the established times for community meals. In fact, if
any are offered something to eat or drink by the superior
and refuse it but then later begin to feel a desire for what
they formerly refused or for anything else, they should
receive nothing at all until they have made due apology.

CHAPTER 44

The reconciliation of those excommunicated

ANY MEMBERS OF THE COMMUNITY WHO HAVE BEEN
excommunicated from the oratory and the refectory for
faults which are really serious must prostrate themselves at
the entrance to the oratory at the time when the celebration
of the work of God comes to an end. They should in
complete silence simply lay their heads on the ground
before the feet of all the community coming out of the
oratory and stay there until the superior judges that they
have done enough in reparation. When called they should
rise and prostrate themselves first of all at the feet of the
superior and then of all the community to beg their
prayers. After that they should be received back into the
choir in whatever order the superior decides. However they
should not venture to take the lead in reciting psalms or in
reading or in any other choir duty until they are again
permitted to do so. Indeed at the end of every office they
should prostrate themselves again on the ground in their
place in choir and thus continue their reparation until
permission is given by the superior to give up this
penitential act.

Anyone who is excommunicated from the refectory only for a less serious fault should perform the same act of reparation in the oratory until permitted to cease; the superior brings this penance to an end by giving a blessing and saying 'that is enough'.

⁂

CHAPTER 45

Mistakes in the Oratory

ANYONE WHO MAKES A MISTAKE IN A PSALM, responsory, antiphon or reading must have the humility to make immediate reparation there before all the community in the oratory. A failure to do that so clearly shows lack of the humility to put right a fault which was due to carelessness that it must incur a more severe punishment. Children, however, should be smacked for such faults of careless inattention.

⁂

CHAPTER 46

Faults committed elsewhere

ANY MEMBER OF THE COMMUNITY WHO IN THE course of some work in the kitchen, in the stores, while fulfilling a service to others or in the bakery, the garden or the workshops or anywhere else does something wrong or happens to break or lose something or to be guilty of some other wrongdoing, must as soon as possible appear before the superior and the community with a voluntary admission of the failure and willing reparation for it. If any are guilty of such faults and fail to make such amends immediately and the truth comes out in another way then the guilty should be punished more severely.

It is, however, important that, if the cause of wrongdoing lies in a sinful secret of conscience, it should be revealed only to the superior or one of those in the community with recognized spiritual experience and understanding, who will know the way to the healing of their own wounds and those of others without exposing them in public.

CHAPTER 47

Signalling the times for the work of God

THE SUPERIOR IS PERSONALLY RESPONSIBLE FOR making sure that the time for the work of God, both at night and during the daytime, is clearly made known to all. This may, of course, be done by delegating the duty to a responsible member of the community, who can be relied on to make sure that everything is done at the proper time.

The superior, followed by other authorized members of the community in their due order, should give a lead by intoning psalms and antiphons for the choir. Only those, however, should come forward to sing and read who have the ability to fulfil this role in a way which is helpful to others. All must play their part under the directions of the superior with humility and restraint and out of reverence to God.

CHAPTER 48

Daily manual labour

IDLENESS IS THE ENEMY OF THE SOUL. THEREFORE all the community must be occupied at definite times in manual labour and at other times in *lectio divina*.* We propose the following arrangements, then, to cater for both these needs.

From Easter to the first of October they will go out in the morning from after Prime until the fourth hour and work at whatever needs to be done. The period from the fourth

---

* *Lectio divina* for St Benedict meant careful and attentive reading of the scriptures and of other sacred writings especially the monastic Fathers. It was done with a conscious openness of heart to the Holy Spirit who was perceived to be speaking to the individual through the sacred text; it was thus closely linked to prayer and became a primary source of spiritual growth. *Lectio* also involved learning by heart the psalms and other passages of scripture. It was this discipline of *lectio* that gave rise in the dark times that were to come to the emergence of Benedictine monasteries as centres of literacy and of learning in scripture and theology. That learning was thorough but never exclusively intellectual, because openness of mind and heart were integral to the discipline of *lectio* which was always faithfully cherished in the monasteries. It led them in due course to go beyond St Benedict's immediate perspective and to embrace the riches of classical literature and learning which they, together with the Irish monasteries in Europe, did so much to preserve from oblivion through monastic *scriptoria*. Justice cannot be done to all this in a brief note. It is enough to say here that the *lectio divina* to which St Benedict refers in this chapter became the basis and source of all Benedictine education, both religious and secular, and is still perhaps its most precious inspiration in an age so threatened by the barriers of narrow specialization in everything.

hour until about the sixth hour should be given to *lectio divina*. After Sext when they have finished their meal they should rest in complete silence on their beds. If anyone wants to read at that time it should be done so quietly that it does not disturb anyone. The office of None could then be a little early coming half way through the eighth hour after which any work which is necessary should be attended to until Vespers. It may be, of course, that because of local conditions or the poverty of the monastery the community may themselves have to do the harvest work. If that happens it should not discourage anyone because they will really be in the best monastic tradition if the community is supported by the work of their own hands. It is just what our fathers did and the apostles themselves. Nevertheless there must always be moderation in whatever such demands are made on the community to protect those who have not a strong constitution.

From the first of October to the beginning of Lent they should devote themselves to *lectio divina* until the end of the second hour, at which time they gather for Terce and then they work at the tasks assigned to them until the ninth hour.* At the first signal for the ninth hour they must all put aside their work so as to be ready for the second signal. Then after the community meal they will spend their time in reading or learning the psalms.

There will be a different arrangement for the time of Lent. The morning will be given to reading until the end of the third hour and then until the end of the tenth hour they

---

* Note on 'hours' in the Rule. For the Romans, each day (from dawn to dusk) and each night (from dusk to dawn) was divided into twelve 'hours'. The actual length of these 'hours' varied according to the season; in summer they were longer during the day and shorter at night, but in winter they were shorter during the day and longer at night. Only at the two equinoxes did the actual length of the hours even out. Timekeeping, therefore, called for a special expertise and flexibility.

will work at their assigned tasks. As a special provision during these days of Lent each member of the community is to be given a book from the library to read thoroughly each day in a regular and conscientious way. These books should be handed out at the beginning of Lent.

It is very important that one or two seniors should be assigned to the task of doing the rounds of the monastery during any of the periods when the community is engaged in reading. They should make sure that there is no one overcome by idle boredom and wasting time in gossip instead of concentrating on the reading before them. Such a one is also a distraction to others. Any of the community who are discovered – which God forbid – to be guilty of such behaviour should be corrected on the first and second occasion. If there is no improvement then they should be given a punishment, in accordance with the Rule, which will act as a deterrent to others. Of course, it is always wrong for members of the community to associate with each other at times when this is not appropriate.

Sunday is the day on which all should be occupied in *lectio divina*, except for those who are assigned to particular duties. If there are any who are so feckless and lazy that they have become unwilling or unable any longer to study or read seriously then they must be given suitable work which is within their powers so that they may not sink into idleness.

As for those who are sick or too frail for demanding work, they should be given the sort of work or craft which will save them from idleness but not burden them with physical work that is beyond their strength. The superior should show understanding concern for their limitations.

CHAPTER 49

How Lent should be observed in the monastery

THERE CAN BE NO DOUBT THAT MONASTIC LIFE
should always have a Lenten character about it, but there
are not many today who have the strength for that.
Therefore we urge that all in the monastery during these
holy days of Lent should look carefully at the integrity of
their lives and get rid in this holy season of any thoughtless
compromises which may have crept in at other times. We
can achieve this as we should if we restrain ourselves from
bad habits of every kind and at the same time turn
wholeheartedly to the prayer of sincere contrition, to *lectio
divina*, to heartfelt repentance and to self-denial. So during
Lent let us take on some addition to the demands of our
accustomed service of the Lord such as special prayers and
some sacrifice of food and drink. Thus each one of us may
have something beyond the normal obligations of monastic
life to offer freely to the Lord with the joy of the Holy
Spirit[1] by denying our appetites through giving up
something from our food or drink or sleep or from
excessive talking and loose behaviour so as to increase the
joy of spiritual longing with which we should look forward
to the holy time of Easter.

Everyone should, of course, submit the details of these
personal offerings for Lent to the superior for approval and
a blessing. This is important; any individual obligation
undertaken in the monastery without the permission of the
superior will be accounted the result of presumption and
vainglory so that no reward can be expected for it.
Everything undertaken in the monastery must have the
approval of the superior.

CHAPTER 50

Those whose work takes them away from the monastery

THOSE WHOSE WORK TAKES THEM SOME DISTANCE from the monastery so that they cannot manage to get to the oratory at the right times for prayer must kneel with profound reverence for the Lord and perform the work of God at their place of work. It is for the superior to make the decision that this is necessary and appropriate.

In the same way those sent on a journey must be careful not to omit the hours of prayer which are prescribed for the whole community. They must observe them in the best way they can so as not to neglect the service they owe the Lord by their profession.

CHAPTER 51

Those on local errands or work

ANY WHO ARE SENT ON AN ERRAND WHICH WILL allow them to return to the monastery on the same day must not eat outside, in spite of pressing invitations whatever their source, unless the superior has approved this. The penalty for infringement of this principle will be excommunication.

CHAPTER 52

The oratory of the monastery

THE ORATORY MUST BE SIMPLY A PLACE OF PRAYER, as the name itself implies, and it must not be used for any other activities at all nor as a place for storage of any kind. At the completion of the work of God all must depart in absolute silence which will maintain a spirit of reverence towards the Lord so that anyone wishing to pray alone in private may not be prevented by the irreverent behaviour of another. Then also anyone who at some other time wants to pray privately may very simply go into the oratory and pray secretly, not in a loud voice but with tears of devotion that come from the heart. That is why, as I have said, those who do not share this purpose are not permitted to stay in the oratory after the end of any Office for fear of interfering with the prayers of others.

CHAPTER 53

The reception of guests

ANY GUEST WHO HAPPENS TO ARRIVE AT THE monastery should be received just as we would receive Christ himself, because he promised that on the last day he will say: I was a stranger and you welcomed me.[1] Proper respect should be shown to everyone while a special welcome is reserved for those who are of the household of our Christian faith[2] and for pilgrims.

74

As soon as the arrival of a guest is announced, the superior and members of the community should hurry to offer a welcome with warm-hearted courtesy. First of all, they should pray together so as to seal their encounter in the peace of Christ. Prayer should come first and then the kiss of peace, so to evade any delusions which the devil may contrive.

Guests should always be treated with respectful deference. Those attending them both on arrival and departure should show this by a bow of the head or even a full prostration on the ground which will leave no doubt that it is indeed Christ who is received and venerated in them. Once guests have been received they should be invited to pray and then to sit down with the superior or whoever is assigned to this duty. Then some sacred scripture should be read for the spiritual encouragement it brings us, and after that every mark of kindness should be shown the guests. The rules of a fast day may be broken by the superior to entertain guests, unless it is a special day on which the fast cannot be broken, but the rest of the community should observe all the fasts as usual. The superior pours water for the guests to wash their hands and then washes their feet with the whole community involved in the ceremony. Then all recite this verse: Lord we have received your mercy in the very temple that is yours.

The greatest care should be taken to give a warm reception to the poor and to pilgrims, because it is in them above all others that Christ is welcomed. As for the rich, they have a way of exacting respect through the very fear inspired by the power they wield.

The kitchen to serve the superior together with the guests should be quite separate, so that guests, who are never lacking in a monastery, may not unsettle the community by arriving, as they do, at all times of the day. Two competent members of the community should serve in this kitchen for a year at a time. They should be given assistants whenever they need it, so as to have no cause for murmuring* in their service. When the pressure from guests dies down the assistants can then be moved to other work assigned them. Of course, it is not only for those serving in the kitchen for superior and guests that this principle should obtain. It should be a guideline for all the duties in the monastery that relief should be made available when it is needed and then, when the need is over, the assistants should obediently move to whatever other work is assigned them.

The accommodation for the guests should be furnished with suitable beds and bedding and one God-fearing member of the community should also be assigned to look after them. The monastery is a house of God and should always be wisely administered by those who are wise themselves. No member of the community should associate in any way or have speech with guests without permission. If they should meet guests or see them it would be right to greet them with deep respect, as we have said; then after asking a blessing they should move on explaining that they may not enter into conversation with guests.

CHAPTER 54

The reception of letters and gifts in the monastery

NO ONE IN A MONASTIC COMMUNITY MAY RECEIVE or send to others letters, gifts of piety or any little tokens without the permission of the superior, whether it is their

* See note in Chapter 5.

parents who are concerned or anyone else at all or another member of the community. Even if their parents send them a present they must not decide for themselves to accept without first referring the matter to the superior. Then it will be for the superior, after agreeing to the reception of the gift, to decide who in the community should receive the gift and, if it is not the one to whom it was sent, that should not give rise to recriminations lest the devil be given an opportunity.[1] Anyone who infringes these principles must be corrected by the discipline of the Rule.

CHAPTER 55

Clothing and footwear for the community

THE LOCAL CONDITIONS AND CLIMATE SHOULD BE the deciding factors in questions about the clothing of the community, because obviously in a cold climate more clothing is needed and less where it is warm. The superior must give careful thought to these questions. However my suggestion for temperate regions is that each member of the community should receive a cowl and tunic, a scapular to wear at work and both sandals and shoes as footwear. The cowl should be thick and warm in winter but of thinner or well-worn material in summer. The community must not be too sensitive about the colour and quality of this clothing; they should be content with what is available in the locality at a reasonable cost. However the superior should see to it that the garments are not short and ill-fitting but appropriate to the size and build of those who wear them.

When new clothing is issued, the old should be immediately
returned to be put in store for distribution to the poor.
Two tunics and cowls should be enough for each member
of the community to provide for night-wear and for
laundering. Anything more than that would be excessive
and this must be avoided. Sandals also and other articles
which are worn out should be handed in when new ones
are issued. Underclothing for those going on a journey
should be provided from the community wardrobe which,
on their return, should be washed and handed in again.
Then there should be cowls and tunics available of slightly
better quality than usual, which may be issued to travellers
from the wardrobe and restored there on their return.

For bedding a mat, a woollen blanket, a coverlet and a pillow
should be enough. The superior ought to inspect the beds at
regular intervals to see that private possessions are not being
hoarded there. If anyone is found with something for which
no permission has been given by the superior, this fault must
be punished with real severity. In order to root out completely
this vice of hoarding personal possessions, the superior must
provide all members of the community with whatever they
really need, that is: cowl, tunic, sandals, shoes, belt, knife,
stylus, needle, handkerchief and writing tablets. Every excuse
about what individuals need will thus be removed.

There is one saying, however, from the Acts of the Apostles
which the superior must always bear in mind, namely that
proper provision was made according to the needs of each.[1]
It is on these grounds that the superior should take into
account what is truly necessary for those who suffer from
an individual weakness, while ignoring the ill will of the
envious, and in every decision remembering that an account
must be given of it in the future judgement of God.

CHAPTER 56

The table for the superior and community guests

THE SUPERIOR'S TABLE SHOULD ALWAYS BE WITH
the guests and pilgrims. In the absence of guests members
of the community, invited by the superior, may take their
place but one or two seniors should always be left with the
community to keep an eye on standards of behaviour.

※

CHAPTER 57

Members of the community with creative gifts

IF THERE ARE ANY IN THE COMMUNITY WITH
creative gifts, they should use them in their workshops with
proper humility, provided that they have the permission of
the superior. If any of them conceive an exaggerated idea of
their competence in this sort of work, imagining that the
value of their work puts the monastery in their debt, they
should be forbidden further exercise of their skills and not
allowed to return to their workshops unless they respond
with humility to this rebuke and the superior permits them
to resume their work.

If any product of the workshops is to be sold, those
responsible for the sale must be careful to avoid any
dishonest practice. They should remember Ananias[1] and
Sapphira who suffered bodily death for their sin, whereas
any who are guilty of fraud in the administration of the

monastery's affairs will suffer death of the soul. In fixing
the prices for these products care should be taken to avoid
any taint of avarice. What is asked by the monastery
should be somewhat lower than the price demanded by
secular workshops so that God may be glorified in
everything.[2]

⁂

CHAPTER 58

The reception of candidates for the community

THE ENTRY OF POSTULANTS INTO THE MONASTIC LIFE
should not be made too easy, but we should follow
St John's precept to make trial of the spirits to see if they
are from God.[1] If, then, a newcomer goes on knocking at
the door and after four or five days has given sufficient
evidence of patient perseverance and does not waver from
the request for entry but accepts the rebuffs and difficulties
put in the way, then let a postulant with that strength of
purpose be received and given accommodation in the guest
quarters for a few days. Then later the new recruit can be
received among the novices in the quarters where they
study, eat and sleep.

A senior who is skilled at guiding souls should be chosen to
look after the novices and to do so with close attention to
their spiritual development. The first concern for novices
should be to see whether it is God himself that they truly
seek, whether they have a real love for the work of God
combined with a willing acceptance of obedience and of
any demands on their humility and patience that monastic
life may make on them. They should not be shielded from

any of the trials of monastic life which can appear to us to be hard and even harsh as they lead us on our way to God.

If novices after two months show promise of remaining faithful in stability, they should have the whole of this Rule read to them and then be faced with this challenge at the end: that is the law under which you ask to serve; if you can be faithful to it, enter; if you cannot, then freely depart. Those who still remain firm in their intention should be led back to the novitiate so that their patience may be further tested. After another six months the Rule should again be read to them so as to remove all doubt about what they propose to undertake. If they still remain firm, then after four more months the same Rule should again be read to them. By that stage they have had plenty of time to think it all over and, if they promise to observe everything and to be faithful to anything that obedience may demand they should be received into the community. Of course, they must by now be fully aware that from that day forward there can be no question of their leaving the monastery nor of shaking off the yoke of the Rule, which in all that time of careful deliberation they were quite free to turn away from or to accept as their way of life.

When the decision is made that novices are to be accepted, then they come before the whole community in the oratory to make solemn promise of stability, fidelity to monastic life and obedience. The promise is made before God and the saints and the candidates must reflect that, if they ever by their actions deny what they have promised, they will be condemned by the God they have betrayed. Novices must record their promises in a document in the name of the saints whose relics are there in the oratory and also in the name of their abbot or abbess in whose presence the promise is made. Each must write the document in his or her own hand or, if unable to write, ask another to write it instead; then, after adding a personal signature or mark to the document, each must place it individually on the altar. As the record lies on the altar they intone this verse: 'Receive me, O Lord, in accordance with your word and I shall live, and do not disappoint me in the hope that you have given me.'[2] The whole community will repeat this verse three times and add at the end the *Gloria Patri.* Each novice then prostrates before every member of the community asking their prayers and from that day is counted as a full member of the community.

Before making their profession novices should give any possessions they may have either to the poor or to the monastery in a formal document keeping back for themselves nothing at all in the full knowledge that from that day they retain no power over anything – not even over their own bodies. As a sign of this the newly professed in the oratory immediately after the promises discard their own clothing and are clothed in habits belonging to the monastery. Their lay clothes are kept safely in case – which God forbid – any should listen to the enticements of the devil and leave the monastery discarding the monastic habit as they are dismissed from the community. The record of their profession, however, which the superior took from the altar should not be returned but should be preserved in the monastery.

CHAPTER 59

Children offered by nobles or by the poor

IF PARENTS WHO ARE FROM THE NOBILITY WANT TO offer to God in the monastery one of their children, who is too young to take personal responsibility, they should draw up a document like that described above and, as they make the offering, wrap the document with the child's hand in the altar cloth.

As to questions of property, they should add a promise to the document under oath that they will not themselves, nor through any other person, give the child anything at any time, nor yet contrive any opportunity whereby the child might be able in the future to acquire possessions. If they are unwilling to do this and insist on making a gift to the monastery and so merit a reward from God, they should draw up a form of donation transferring the property in question to the monastery keeping, if they wish, the revenue for themselves. Everything concerned with this property should be negotiated in such a way that not the slightest hint of personal expectations can be entertained by the child in a way which could lead through deception to ruin. Experience has shown how this can happen.

Poor people may make the offering of a child in the same way. If they have no property at all, they simply write and offer the child with the document in the presence of witnesses.

CHAPTER 60

The admission of priests into the monastery

AN ORDAINED PRIEST WHO ASKS TO BE RECEIVED into the monastery should not be accepted too quickly. If, however, he shows real perseverance in his request, he must understand that, if accepted, he will be bound to observe the full discipline of the Rule and may expect no relaxations. He will have to face up to the scriptural question: friend what have you come here for?[1] He should be allowed, however, to take his place after the abbot and exercise his ministry in giving blessings and offering Mass, provided that the abbot allows it.

He must understand that he is subject to the requirements of the Rule. He must not make any special demands but rather give everyone else an example of humility. If any question of rank arises in the community on the score of ordination or any other matter, he must take the place determined by the date of his entry into the community not by any concession granted through reverence for his priesthood. If anyone in one of the orders of clerics asks to join the monastery, the right place will be somewhere about the middle of the community, but they too are required to make the promises about observing the Rule and monastic stability.

⁂

CHAPTER 61

Monastic pilgrims from far away

MONKS OR NUNS ON A PILGRIMAGE FROM FAR AWAY, who come to the monastery asking to be received as guests, should be received for as long as they wish to stay, provided that they are content with the local style of life they encounter and cause no disturbance in the monastery by any excess in personal behaviour. It may happen, of course, that one of them may find something to point out in criticism about the customs of the monastery, using sound arguments in a spirit of charitable deference. In that case the superior should consider the whole question with care and prudence in case it was for this very purpose that the pilgrim was sent by the Lord. Then, if later such a pilgrim wishes to embrace stability in the monastery, the request should not meet with automatic refusal, especially since it will have been possible to discern the qualities of the new postulant while still a guest.

If, on the other hand, such a pilgrim monk or nun has been revealed as a guest to be overbearing and full of bad habits then not only should all further association with the community be refused but such a guest should quite openly be requested to depart for fear that such a wretched example might lead others astray. But if no such negative signs are apparent it may be right to go further and not wait for a request to be accepted in the community. It may even be right to persuade such a one to stay so that others may benefit and learn from such example. After all, in all the world there is only one Lord and one King in whose service we are all engaged to fight. The superior may even perceive qualities in such a pilgrim to suggest that it would be right to grant a somewhat higher position in the community order than would be justified merely by the date of entry. The same principle would apply also to a postulant from the orders of priests and clerics, who have been mentioned above. The superior may decide to place one of them in a position higher than that dictated by the date of their entry, if he sees that their monastic observance is worthy of it.

The abbot or abbess, however, must be careful not to accept to stay as a guest any monk or nun from another known monastery without the consent of the appropriate superior and a letter of commendation. They must bear in mind the warning of scripture: do not do to another what you would not wish to suffer yourself.[1]

CHAPTER 62

The priors of the monastery

IF AN ABBOT WISHES TO HAVE A MONK ORDAINED
priest or deacon he must select one from his community
who has the gifts needed for the priesthood. When
ordained a monk must be careful to avoid a spirit of
self-importance or pride and he must avoid taking on
himself any duties to which the abbot has not assigned him.
He must be amenable to the discipline of the Rule, all the
more because of his priesthood. His ordination to the
priesthood should be no occasion for him to be forgetful of
obedience and the obligations of the Rule, but he must
more and more direct the growth of his spiritual life
towards the Lord. He must keep his place in community
order according to the date of his coming to the monastery
except in his priestly duties at the altar and unless by the
will of the community and with the approval of the abbot
he is promoted because of the good example of his
monastic observance.

He must in any case be faithful to the principles laid down
for the deans and the prior of the monastery. If he should
be headstrong enough to behave in any other way, he will
be accounted not a priest but a rebel and treated
accordingly. If he ignores repeated warnings and does not
reform, the evidence of this must be brought before the
Bishop. If even that brings no improvement and his
offences become notorious, he will have to be dismissed
from the monastery, but that must be avoided unless he is
so arrogant that he refuses to submit and obey.

CHAPTER 63

Community order

THE THREE CRITERIA FOR THE ORDER OF
precedence in the community are first of all the date of
entry, then monastic observance and the decision of the
abbot or abbess. But they must not cause unrest in the
flocks committed to them by acting unjustly and as though
with arbitrary authority but must remember at all times
that an account will have to be given of all their decisions
and works in this world. Well then, whenever the
community gets into order for the kiss of peace, or for
Holy Communion or for intoning the psalms or taking
their place in choir or in any other circumstances they
must be guided by the superior's directions or the order
established by the date of their entry. Age must never be
the deciding factor in community order just as it was that
Samuel and Daniel judged their elders when they were still
only boys.[1] So, apart from those whom the superior has
promoted for a more cogent reason or demoted for specific
faults, all the others retain the order of their conversion
to monastic life so exactly that one who arrived at the
monastery door at the second hour must accept a place
junior to another who came an hour earlier, whatever their
age or former rank may have been. Children, of course,
must be kept in their subordinate place by everyone on all
occasions.

Juniors in the community should show due respect for their
seniors, and seniors should love and care for their juniors.
When they address each other it should not be simply by
name, but senior monks call their juniors 'brother' and the
juniors address their seniors as 'nonnus' or 'reverend
father'. The abbot is understood to hold the place of Christ

in the monastery and for this reason is called 'lord' or 'abbot', not because he demands it for himself but out of reverence and love of Christ;* it is a point on which he should often reflect to help him to live up to so great an honour.

When members of a monastic community meet each other, the junior asks a blessing of the senior. As a senior passes by, the junior rises and yields a place for the senior to sit down and will never sit without the senior's permission. In that way they will conform to scripture which says they should try to be the first to show respect for each other.[2] Small children and adolescents must keep their places in the oratory and the refectory in a disciplined way. Anywhere else, and especially outside the monastery, they must be under supervision and control until they have learnt responsibility as they get older.

⁂

CHAPTER 64

The election of an abbot or abbess

IN THE PROCESS THROUGH WHICH AN ABBOT OR abbess is elected the principle to be borne in mind is that the one finally elected should be the choice of the whole community acting together in the fear of God or else of a small group in the community, however small they may be in numbers, provided they have sounder judgement. The grounds on which a candidate is elected abbot or abbess must

---

* For the same reasons an abbess is called 'lady abbess' and nuns in a monastic community address each other as 'sister' or 'mother'.

be the quality of their monastic life and the wisdom of their teaching, even if they are the last in order in the community.

If it should happen – and may God forbid it – that the whole community should conspire to elect one who will consent to their evil way of life, and if their corrupt ways become known to the bishop of the local diocese or to the abbots or abbesses or ordinary Christians living nearby, they should intervene to prevent so depraved a conspiracy and provide for the appointment of a worthy guardian for the house of God. They may be sure that they will receive a rich reward for this good act, if it is done out of pure intentions and zeal for the Lord, while if they neglect to intervene in such a situation it will be accounted sinful.

The abbot or abbess, once established in office, must often think about the demands made on them by the burden they have undertaken and consider also to whom they will have to give an account of their stewardship.[1] They must understand that the call of their office is not to exercise power over those who are their subjects but to serve and help them in their needs. They must be well-grounded in the law of God so that they may have the resources to bring forth what is new and what is old in their teaching.[2] They must be chaste, sober and compassionate and should always let mercy triumph over judgement[3] in the hope of themselves receiving like treatment from the Lord. While they must hate all vice, they must love their brothers or sisters. In correcting faults they must act with prudence being conscious of the danger of breaking the vessel itself by attacking the rust too vigorously. They should always bear their own frailty in mind and remember not to crush the bruised reed.[4] Of course I do not mean that they should allow vices to grow wild but rather use prudence and charity in cutting them out, so as to help each one in their individual needs, as I have already said. They should seek to be loved more than they are feared.

They should not be trouble-makers nor given to excessive anxiety nor should they be too demanding and obstinate, nor yet interfering and inclined to suspicion so as never to be at rest. In making decisions they should use foresight and care in analysing the situation, so that whether they are giving orders about sacred or about secular affairs they should be far-seeing and moderate in their decisions. They might well reflect on the discretion of the holy patriarch Jacob when he said: if I force my flock to struggle further on their feet, they will all die in a single day.[5] They should take to heart these and other examples of discretion, the mother of virtues, and manage everything in the monastery so that the strong may have ideals to inspire them and the weak may not be frightened away by excessive demands. Above all they must remain faithful to this Rule in every detail, so that after fulfilling their ministry well they may hear the words uttered to that good servant who provided bread for fellow servants at the proper time: I tell you solemnly the Lord sets his faithful servant over all that he possesses.[6]

CHAPTER 65

The prior or prioress of the monastery

IT HAS OFTEN HAPPENED THAT UNFORTUNATE conflicts have arisen in monasteries as a result of the appointment of a prior or prioress as second in authority to the superior. There have been instances when some of these officials have conceived out of an evil spirit of self-importance that they also are superiors and for that reason have assumed the powers of a tyrant, so that they encourage scandalous divisions in the community. This sort of thing is most likely to happen in those regions where the prior or prioress is appointed by the same bishop or priest who appointed the abbot or abbess. It is clear how very foolish this arrangement is, because it provides the grounds for these subordinate officials to think proudly from the very beginning that they are exempt from the superior's authority on the specious grounds that their own authority derives from the same source as their superior's. That simply encourages the development of envy, quarrels, slander, rivalry, divisions and disorderly behaviour. The result is that, because of the conflict between the superior and the second in command, their own souls are at risk and their subjects take sides in the dispute, which brings ruin on them too. The responsibility for this and all the danger and evil it brings rests on the heads of those who devised such a confusing method of appointment.

We have no doubt, therefore, that it is best in the interests of preserving peace and charity that the authority for the whole administration of the monastery should rest with the abbot or abbess. If possible, as noted above, it is best that everything should be organized through deans according to the wishes of the superior. Then, since power is delegated to many, there is no room for pride to take hold of any individual. However, if local needs suggest it and if the community makes the request with good reason and deference and the superior thinks it the right course to follow, the superior should take counsel with God-fearing seniors and appoint a second in command. Then the prior or prioress so appointed must carry out the duties delegated to them with due respect for the superior, against whose expressed wishes nothing must be attempted by them. The higher the position thus conferred on anyone the greater must be his or her devotion to the observance of the Rule.

If the prior or prioress is subsequently found to be led astray
by pride into serious faults and shows scant respect for the
holy Rule, then up to four times they must be rebuked in
words. If there is no improvement the discipline of the
Rule must be applied. If that brings no improvement, then
there is nothing for it but dismissal from this position so
that another more worthy candidate may be promoted.
If a dismissed prior or prioress cannot live in peace and
obedience in the community, then they must be expelled
from the monastery. But the superior must take care not to
be seared in soul by the flames of jealousy or envy and to
remember always the account we shall have to give to God
of all the judgements we make.

CHAPTER 66

The porter or portress of the monastery

AT THE ENTRANCE TO THE MONASTERY THERE
should be a wise senior who is too mature in stability to
think of wandering about and who can deal with enquiries
and give whatever help is required. This official's room
should be near the main door so that visitors will always
find someone there to greet them. As soon as anyone
knocks on the door or one of the poor calls out, the
response, uttered at once with gentle piety and warm
charity, should be 'thanks be to God' or 'your blessing,
please'. If the porter or portress needs help, then a junior
should be assigned to this task.

The monastery itself should be constructed so as to include
within its bounds all the facilities which will be needed,

that is water, a mill, a garden and workshops for various crafts. Then there will be no need for monks and nuns to wander outside which is far from good for their monastic development. We intend that this Rule should be read at regular intervals in the community so that no one may have the excuse of ignorance.

❦

CHAPTER 67

Those who are sent on a journey

THOSE WHO ARE SENT ON A JOURNEY SHOULD commend themselves to the prayers of all the community as well as of the superior and, at the last prayer of the work of God in the oratory, there should always be a memento of all who may be absent. Any who come back from a journey should lie prostrate in the oratory at the end of each of the Hours to ask the prayer of the whole community in case they have chanced to suffer any harm from what they have seen or heard or from idle gossip on their journey. None of them should be foolish enough to give an account to anyone in the community of what they may have seen or heard while away from the monastery, because this can do much harm. If any dare to do so they must receive the punishment of the Rule. The same must apply to anyone who presumes to go outside the enclosure of the monastery or to go anywhere or do anything, however small, without the superior's permission.

❦

CHAPTER 68

The response to orders that seem impossible

IF INSTRUCTIONS ARE GIVEN TO ANYONE IN THE
community which seem too burdensome or even impossible,
then the right thing is to accept the order in a spirit of
uncomplaining obedience. However, if the burden of this
task appears to be completely beyond the strength of the
monk or nun to whom it has been assigned, then there
should be no question of a rebellious or proud rejection,
but it would be quite right to choose a good opportunity
and point out gently to the superior the reasons for
thinking that the task is really impossible. If the superior
after listening to this submission still insists on the original
command, then the junior must accept that it is the right
thing and with loving confidence in the help of God obey.

CHAPTER 69

No one should act as advocate for another

GREAT CARE MUST BE TAKEN TO AVOID ANY
tendency for one of the community to take the side of and
try to protect another, even though they may be closely
related through ties of blood. Such a thing must not happen
in the monastery because it would provide a very serious
occasion of scandal. Anyone who acts against this principle
must be sharply deterred by punishment.

CHAPTER 70

The offence of striking another

EVERY OCCASION FOR PRESUMPTUOUS BEHAVIOUR IN
a monastery must be avoided, so we insist that no one in the
community may excommunicate or strike another unless
given the power to do so by the superior. Those guilty of such
wrongdoing should be rebuked before everyone so that all
others may fear.[1] Everyone, however, should have some
responsibility for the control and supervision of children up
to the age of fifteen, but they must be moderate and sensible
in the way they exercise it. Just as among the adults any who
assume power over others must be punished so anyone who
flares up immoderately against children must be subjected to
the discipline of the Rule, for it is written in scripture; do not
do to another what you would be unwilling to suffer
yourself.[2]

CHAPTER 71

Mutual obedience in the monastery

OBEDIENCE IS OF SUCH VALUE THAT IT SHOULD BE
shown not only to the superior but all members of the
community should be obedient to each other in the sure
knowledge that this way of obedience is the one that will
take them straight to God. Of course any commands from
the abbot or abbess or those they have delegated must take
precedence and cannot be over-ridden by unofficial orders,

but when that has been said, all juniors should obey their seniors showing them love and concern. Anyone objecting to this should be corrected.

Any monk or nun who is corrected for anything by abbot or abbess or one of the seniors and perceives that the senior is upset by feelings of anger, even though they may be well in control, then that junior should at once prostrate on the ground in contrition and not move until the senior gives a blessing which will heal the upset. Anyone who disdains to do so should receive corporal punishment or in a case of real rebellion be expelled from the monastery.

CHAPTER 72

The good spirit which should inspire monastic life

IT IS EASY TO RECOGNIZE THE BITTER SPIRIT OF wickedness which creates a barrier to God's grace and opens the way to the evil of hell. But equally there is a good spirit which frees us from evil ways and brings us closer to God and eternal life. It is this latter spirit that all who follow the monastic way of life should strive to cultivate, spurred on by fervent love. By following this path they try to be first to show respect to one another with the greatest patience in tolerating weaknesses of body or character. They should even be ready to outdo each other in mutual obedience so that no one in the monastery aims at personal advantage but is rather concerned for the good of others.[1] Thus the pure love of one another as of one family should be their ideal. As for God they should have a profound and loving reverence for him. They should love their abbot or abbess with sincere and unassuming affection. They should value nothing whatever above Christ himself and may he bring us all together to eternal life.

＊

CHAPTER 73

This Rule is only a beginning

THE PURPOSE FOR WHICH WE HAVE WRITTEN THIS rule is to make it clear that by observing it in our monasteries we can at least achieve the first steps in virtue and good monastic practice. Anyone, however, who wishes to press on towards the highest standards of monastic life may turn to the teachings of the holy Fathers, which can lead those who follow them to the very heights of perfection. Indeed, what page, what saying from the sacred scriptures of the Old and New Testaments is not given us by the authority of God as reliable guidance for our lives on earth? Then there are the Conferences and the Institutes and the Lives of the Fathers and the rule of our holy father Basil. What else are these works but the means of true progress in virtue for those aiming at high standards of observance and obedience in monastic life? We, however, can only blush with shame when we reflect on the negligence and inadequacy of the monastic lives we lead.

Whoever you may be, then, in your eagerness to reach your Father's home in heaven, be faithful with Christ's help to this small Rule which is only a beginning. Starting from there you may in the end aim at the greater heights of monastic teaching and virtue in the works which we have mentioned above and with God's help you will then be able to reach those heights yourself. Amen.

Notes

Prologue

1 Rom. 13:11
2 Ps. 94(95):8
3 Rev. 2:7
4 Ps. 33(34):11
5 John 12:35
6 Ps. 33(34):12
7 Ps. 33(34):13–14
8 Isa. 58:9
9 Ps. 14(15):1
10 Ps. 14(15):2–3
11 Ps. 14(15):4 &
   cf Ps. 136(137):9
12 Ps. 113:9 (Ps. 115:1)
13 1 Cor. 15:10
14 2 Cor. 10:17
15 Matt. 7:24–25
16 Rom. 2:4
17 Ezek. 33:11

Chapter 2

1 Rom. 8:15
2 Ps. 39(40):10; Isa. 1:2
3 Ps. 49(50):16–17
4 Matt. 7:3
5 *cf* Rom. 2:11
6 *cf* 2 Tim. 4:2
7 1 Kings 2:27; 1 Sam. 2:27–36
8 Prov. 18:2
9 Prov. 23:14
10 Luke 12:48
11 Matt. 6:33
12 Ps. 33(34):10

Chapter 3

1 Ecclus. 32:24

Chapter 4

1 Gal. 5:16
2 Matt. 23:3
3 Matt. 5:44–45; Eph. 4:26
4 1 Cor. 2:9

Chapter 5

1 Ps. 17(18):44
2 Luke 10:16
3 Matt. 7:14
4 John 6:38
5 Luke 10:16
6 2 Cor. 9:7

Chapter 6

1 Ps. 38(39):1–2
2 Prov. 10:19
3 Prov. 18:21

Chapter 7

1 Luke 14:11
2 Ps. 130(131):1
3 Ps. 130(131):2. In this case, as in many others, the Latin translation available to St Benedict differed from the original Hebrew and therefore from modern translations of the same. To accept the Latin translator's interpretation is necessary if we are to make some sense of St Benedict's comment.
4 Gen. 28:12
5 Ps. 7:9
6 Ps. 93(94):11
7 Ps. 138(139):2

8 Ps. 75(76):10
9 Ps. 17(18):23
10 Ecclus. 18:30
11 Prov. 16:25
12 Ps. 13(14):1
13 Ps. 37(38):9
14 Ecclus. 18:30
15 Ps. 13(14):2
16 Ps. 49(50):21
17 John 6:38
18 *cf* 2 Tim. 4:8; Rev. 2:10
19 Phil. 2:8
20 Matt. 10:22
21 Ps. 26(27):14
22 Ps. 43(44):22; Rom. 8:36
23 Rom. 8:37
24 Ps. 65(66):10–11
25 *Ibid.* 12
26 Matt. 5:39–41
27 *cf* 1 Cor. 4:12
28 Ps. 36(37):5
29 Ps. 105(106):1
30 Ps. 31(32):5
31 Ps. 72(73):22–23
32 Ps. 21(22):6
33 Ps. 87(88):16
34 Ps. 118(119):71
35 Prov. 10:19
36 Ps. 139(140):11
37 Ecclus. 21:20
38 Luke 18:13
39 Ps. 37(38):6

Chapter 9

1 Ps. 50(51):15

Chapter 13

1 Matt. 6:13

Chapter 16

1 Ps. 118(119):164
2 Ps. 118(119):62
3 Ps. 118(119):164

Chapter 19

1 Ps. 2:11
2 Ps. 46(47):7
3 Ps. 137(138):1

Chapter 25

1 1 Cor. 5:5

Chapter 27

1 Matt. 9:12
2 2 Cor. 2:7–8
3 Ezek. 34:3–4

Chapter 28

1 1 Cor. 5:13
2 1 Cor. 7:15

Chapter 31

1 1 Tim. 3:13
2 Ecclus. 18:16
3 Matt. 18:6

Chapter 33

1 Acts 4:32

Chapter 34

1 Acts 4:35

Chapter 35

1 Ps. 85(86):17
2 Ps. 69(70):1

Chapter 36

1 Matt. 25:36, 40

Chapter 38

1 Ps. 50(51):15

Chapter 39

1 Luke 21:34

Chapter 40

1 1 Cor. 7:7
2 Ecclus. 19:2

Chapter 49

1 *cf* 1 Thess. 1:6

Chapter 53

1 Matt. 25:35
2 Gal. 6:10

Chapter 54

1 Eph. 4:27

Chapter 55

1 Acts 4:35

Chapter 57

1 Acts 5:1–11
2 1 Pet. 4:11

Chapter 58

1 1 John 4:1
2 Ps. 118(119):116

Chapter 60

1 Matt. 26:50

Chapter 61

1 Tobit 4:15

Chapter 63

1 1 Sam. 3:10–18; Dan. 13:44–64
2 Rom. 12:10

Chapter 64

1 Luke 16:2
2 Matt. 13:52
3 Jas. 2:13
4 Isa. 42:3
5 Gen. 33:13
6 Matt. 24:47

Chapter 70

1 1 Tim. 5:20
2 Tobit 4:15

Chapter 72

1 Rom. 12:10

Part Two

Tools of Benedictine Spirituality

The Work of God

One of the most readily recognizable passages in the Rule of St Benedict concerns the public prayer of the monastic community: 'Indeed, nothing is to be preferred to the work of God' (Chapter 43, first paragraph). When Benedict uses such an unusual expression as 'work of God' for the public prayer of the monastery, he is drawing on monastic tradition, where the term probably refers to God's prior claim on human activity as opposed to merely human projects or ambitions.

In any case, Benedict emphasizes the importance of this public prayer by devoting no less than twelve chapters of the Rule to his description of how the 'work of God' is to be structured. He is also very concerned about the timetable for public prayer as he sets aside seven distinct periods during the day when the monks are to drop whatever work may be engaging their attention in order to gather for prayerful recognition of God's claim on their lives.

Time is one of the most precious gifts that we humans receive from God. It is clear that Benedict wants his monks to acknowledge this gift by returning choice portions of their time each day to God. In this way, they will practise the most basic form of hospitality, which is to make room in their schedules for the entertainment of God's real but mysterious presence. All other forms of hospitality, whether it is welcoming guests or respecting nature, derive from this profound respect for the mystery of God. Thus, the apparent folly of 'wasting' time on God becomes the wisest possible use of this precious gift.

This public prayer of the monastic community is made up

primarily of biblical psalms, but there are also readings from other parts of Scripture, as well as special prayers, such as the Lord's Prayer. The constant chanting of the psalms is intended to immerse the monk in a world where God's presence is felt and where God's goodness is praised. This world is made accessible to the monk through personal faith, which finds the gift of God at the centre of all reality, in spite of much evil and violence on the surface of human life.

For the purpose of achieving this prayerful immersion, Benedict prescribed that his monks should memorize the entire Psalter. This must have been a daunting task for the younger members of the monastery. But they would have been greatly assisted and encouraged by the older members, for we can well imagine that they were carried along, as it were, on the waves of biblical words provided by their elders. Over the years, the effect would be that the minds and memories of all the monks would be filled more and more with expressions of praise and gratitude.

Living with the psalms in this way would become like a second nature and would colour the consciousness of the monks in every circumstance of life. This would in turn gradually realize the ideal of monastic holiness, namely, a constant, loving awareness of the reality and presence of God in all of human life. With this awareness would also come a deep inner sense of peace and harmony, regardless of external chaos or even the final disruption we call death.

These unvarying and regular periods of praise and thanksgiving were thus intended to bring about that spiritual conversion which Benedict valued so highly. Such a transformation finds expression ultimately in liberation from self-centred preoccupation and anxiety as the monk commits himself to unselfish love and service. The inner peace and calm realized through prayer will then permit greater awareness of the needs of others and the freedom to respond to those needs.

Such generosity is made possible through an ever-deeper trust in God's goodness as reflected in the reality of divine promises. The future will accordingly be changed from a time of threat and darkness to an illuminated horizon producing invincible hope and joyful expectation. The monastic tradition has recognized this dimension of Benedictine spirituality by making Benedict the patron of a happy death.

It is well worth noting that Benedict, in spite of his meticulous concern for the structure of this public prayer of the community, makes explicit provision for the right of future abbots to modify the timetable and structure of this prayer. This makes it quite clear that Benedict did not believe that an exact, much less a scrupulous, observance of the 'work of God' would produce the salvation of monks in some magical or mechanical way. Such prayerful attention to God will greatly assist them, however, in the painful conversion demanded by unselfish and sensitive behaviour in all areas of their lives.

This public monastic prayer is not to be understood, therefore, as scheduled moments of explicit prayers totally divorced from the rest of the monks' lives. They are to be understood rather as times when God's loving presence is at centre stage, as it were, while at other times of the day God is not totally forgotten but is allowed to recede to the wings. From there his presence can be recalled at any moment, especially when there is that atmosphere of silence and recollection that Benedict wishes his monks to foster in the cloister.

We know that Benedict's spiritual wisdom is valid for all Christians. Many lay people would like to share in that wisdom and they can do so even when they are prevented from regular participation in the public prayer of the monastery. There are breviaries available, which contain prayers very similar to those used in monasteries. By saying these prayers, lay people will also be able to consecrate each day to God and to enter into that same loving awareness of the divine presence in their lives.

Demetrius R. Dumm OSB

The Art of *Lectio Divina*

As it is now used, *lectio divina* is understood as the prayerful meditation on the text of the Bible and of other writings that embody the faith of the Church. The term lectio divina originally referred to the reading of the scriptures during the liturgy. As literacy and the availability of books increased, the context of this reading became less communal and more personal, as can be seen from St Benedict's provision of individual books for reading during Lent. This personal reading served as a complement to the liturgy, and became a characteristic feature of Benedictine spirituality. It ceased to be principally an oral-aural and communal experience and became more and more an internal dialogue of the heart with the text, and through the text with God.

Dynamic

Lectio differs substantially from the ordinary act of reading, even 'spiritual reading'. Lectio is at the service of prayer and goes beyond the act of merely absorbing the contents of a page. The classical formulation of this dynamic was given by Guigo the Carthusian (d. 1188): *lectio, meditatio, oratio, contemplatio*: reading, meditation, prayer, contemplation. What is read must first be digested and assimilated through a process of quiet repetition, in which we aim to become progressively attuned to its subtle echoes in the heart. The text thus serves as a mirror that brings inner realities to consciousness. This heightened awareness exposes our need for divine help and readily leads to prayer.

Sometimes, in this dialogue with God, we become more aware of God than of our own needs and pass into the simpler and more profound state of contemplation. Lectio can thus be viewed as a pathway towards contemplation. This is not, however, to say that the four steps constitute a sequential method to be followed, or that each is present in every lectio. Often the various phases are spread throughout the day as mindfulness of the Word is prolonged, and we keep responding to what we have read in the way that we live.

Practice

Initially we need to acquire the discipline of close reading, paying attention to every word and sentence, and not allowing ourselves to pass over anything. This deliberateness is helped by reading out loud, learning to articulate or vocalize the words as a means of slowing down and avoiding distraction. Lectio is like reading poetry; the sound of the words creates interior assonances, which in turn trigger intuitive connections which lodge more effectively in the memory. In lectio the intention is affective not cognitive, it is a work of a heart that desires to make contact with God and, thereby, to reform our lives.

Some wider reading can help us to sidestep speculative questions which would otherwise disperse our energies. This preparation is not lectio, but it serves it well.

Attention to the ambience of our lectio will often help to lead us more smoothly into prayer. Anything that we can do in terms of choice of place or posture, or to secure silence will keep potential disturbances at bay. Using an icon or a candle, or offering reverence to the book of the scriptures will often help us to move into a more prayerful space.

The Benedictine Spirit

There are three terms found in monastic tradition that describe an appropriate attitude to lectio. Our reading must be assiduous or generous, that is to say it must involve a sustained expenditure of forethought and energy and will often demand a sacrifice of time which could have been devoted to other things. Lectio must be done in a spirit of reverence, expressed in the manner in which we treat the sacred book itself, in our posture and in the way in which we make practical provision to exclude from this space whatever is not sacred. It is reverence which makes us keep silent and receptive so that we can listen to the word that speaks to our souls and brings salvation. When we open the sacred book we also open ourselves; we let ourselves become vulnerable – willing to be pierced by God's two-edged sword. This is what St Benedict refers to as compunction, allowing ourselves to experience the double dynamic of every genuine encounter with God: the growing awareness of our urgent need for forgiveness and healing on the one hand and, on the other, a more profound confidence in God's superabundant mercy.

Challenges

Two areas call for constant vigilance. First we must be not only hearers but doers of the word. Unless we come to our lectio with an antecedent will for conversion, the exercise is vain. Our lectio will thrive most fully when we aim to incarnate what we read in the way we act. When God seems silent, it is usually because either there is a latent resistance, or there is too much inner noise coming from a multiplicity of other concerns. Sometimes the difficulties we experience in lectio serve as a summons to re-examine our lives and to seek to establish there a greater harmony with what we read. Second, we have to renounce the search for novelty. Lectio needs to be regular and not erratic. We need, as St Benedict insisted, to read whole books of Scripture from beginning to end, quietly working our way through a Gospel or an Old Testament prophet, willing to be surprised, resisting the temptation to exercise total control over what we read.

Joy

Lectio demands much of us, but it is an enriching experience that constantly renews our spiritual life. God's word adds perspective to our experience, gives meaning to our struggles and keeps alive the flame of hope. Above all, contact with the scriptures is a source of joy and delight to the heart, bringing us into an ever-deeper relationship to the God whom we seek and to Jesus who calls us.

Michael Casey O CSO

Bibliography

Benedict of Nursia, *Rule for Monasteries*, Ch. 48.
Casey, Michael, *The Art of Sacred Reading*, Dove, Melbourne, 1995.
Casey, Michael, *Sacred Reading*, Triumph Books, Liguori, 1996.
Guigo II, *The Ladder of Monks and Twelve Meditations*, Cistercian Publications, Kalamazoo, 1981, pp. 67–86.

Prayer

Prayer for Benedictines is a relationship with God which opens one to the awareness of God's presence permeating all of one's life. Prayer for ancient monastics was spoken of in terms of *memor Dei* ('remembrance of God'), who is always remembering everything which has been created. Benedict does not present any detailed treatise on personal prayer in his Rule; rather he assumes that prayer derives from the two main monastic practices of formal prayer, that of the *Opus Dei*, or liturgy of hours, and *lectio divina*, the activity of reading, pondering, ruminating and reflecting on the scriptures.

Prayer is an invitation to 'listen with the ear of your heart', the first words of the Prologue that opens the whole Rule of St Benedict. Listening is both a grace given by God and an act of love, for listening requires setting aside one's own preoccupations so as to give oneself time and space to be present to the 'Other'. This 'Other' longs to reveal to us how much we are beloved and to make possible in us our coming to know that we are made in the Divine image and likeness. As one is led more deeply into a relationship with the God whose love is beyond imagining, one is taught by the Spirit how to see every event and person, all creation and happenings from the divine perspective. Gregory the Great describes Benedict's contemplation of 'the whole world . . . brought before his eyes, gathered up, as it were, under a single ray of sun',[1] such that 'the mind of the seer was enlarged: caught up in God, it could see without difficulty all that is under God'.[2] Thus the aim of prayer is that of widening one's vision such that one begins to see as God sees, to love all that God has created as God has, to view life's situations as God does.

How does one come to be such a contemplative? Divine grace makes possible what is not possible by human effort, as the pray-er uncovers the mysteries of the biblical words chanted in the Divine Office and pondered during lectio divina hidden in one's own life. One discovers that the psalms, parables, wisdom sayings, stories and events of Scripture are living words. As they are prayed over under the Spirit's guidance, the particular phrases and scenes become 'real' in one's life. The practice of prayer spills over into the practice of remembering how God is forming the dynamism of those words in one's life. In turn, the living of the words of prayer is manifest in encountering Christ in one's monastic leader, in the community members, in the exchange of hospitality with strangers and guests, and in the service of others in various ministries.

The realization of God's activity in the soul has been expressed in a variety of ways over the centuries, so that prayer forms have changed in response to the larger movements of prayer within differing cultures. In the early centuries of Benedictine life, prayer grew out of the practice of lectio divina, the reading, memorization and contemplation of the Word of God. The phrases which touched the heart during engagement in lectio were carried in the memory and repeatedly considered as the monastic engaged in manual labour. With the Carolingian reform of Charlemagne, monasteries became centres for learning as well as prayer. Those monastics involved in copying manuscripts of the Bible and biblical commentaries in the scriptorium began to portray the fruit of their lectio in illuminations and decorated letters, which, in turn, would serve as material for reflection for others. Commentaries on Scripture multiplied out of a need to explain the scriptures to the people.

As devotion to Mary and the saints began developing in the eleventh and twelfth centuries, along with meditation on Christ's suffering, meditation handbooks became important for those who could read. Prayer books were a means of introducing the educated to reflections drawn from Scripture. Those laity who were unable to read were taught to pray the Lord's Prayer 150 times, a practice which coincided with the praying of 150 psalms of the *Opus Dei* in the monasteries. As devotion to Mary increased in the twelfth century, then *Aves* ('Hail Mary') replaced the 150 *Paters* ('Our Father') and beads were designed to help people visually remember the number of prayers. Along with devotional prayers a flourishing of mystical prayer arose in the high middle ages, often the fruit of pondering the Song of Songs. Commentaries on this biblical book of love poetry abounded in Cistercian and Benedictine monasteries in the twelfth and thirteenth centuries. For example, the influence of the commentaries by Bernard of Clairvaux and William of St Thierry are clearly apparent in the Revelations of Gertrude of Helfta.

As the *devotio moderna* movement spread among the laity in the fourteenth century under the influence of Carthusian monks,[3] the stress on meditation of interior contemplative themes, which were more affective in tone than speculative, also permeated monasteries. Books like Thomas a Kempis' *Imitation of Christ* popularized the practice of twice daily meditations on the life and passion of Christ. Such books of meditations, designed to lead people to interior mental recollection on the mysteries in Christ's life, became over time 'spiritual reading' and often replaced the practice of lectio divina, particularly in women's monasteries of the nineteenth and twentieth centuries prior to the monastic renewal following Vatican Council II.

In the years following Vatican II, study, workshops and publications on lectio divina have brought a return to this practice of Benedictine prayer. In addition, various forms of centring prayer, as taught by John Main OSB, Basil Pennington OCSO and Thomas Keating OCSO, have been a means of attending to the presence of God in contemplative prayer.

Mary Forman OSB

Notes

1 Gregory the Great, *The Life of Saint Benedict*, Commentary by Adalbert de Vogüé, translated by Hilary Costello and Eoin de Bhaldraithe, St Bede's Publications, Petersham, MA, 1993, p. 164.
2 Ibid., p. 165.
3 Peter King, *Western Monasticism: A History of the Monastic Movement in the Latin Church*, Cistercian Studies 185, Cistercian Publications, Kalamazoo, MI/Spencer, MA, 1999, p. 246.

Work*

Working to Rule

What is monastic?

What sort of things do we think are holy? The question seems silly and easy to answer at first. God is holy, so whatever is to do with God is holy too. This leads us very naturally to think about prayer, going to church, acting justly and other spiritual things. All of these are holy and worthwhile, but if we concentrate on them alone, we miss out some very large parts of our lives. Most people spend much of their time working for their living, and working for and within their families. Our daily lives often seem to have nothing holy about them at all. This is a thoroughly un-Christian way of looking at things and the Rule of St Benedict provides something of an antidote.

In Chapter 48 of the Rule, Benedict makes arrangement for the work of the monks. He begins with a remark that has become a proverb, 'Idleness is the enemy of the soul.' He goes on to describe the timetable and anticipates that some communities will be so small or poor that they will have to do quite a lot of work, including bringing in the harvest, by themselves. At this daunting prospect he says, 'Let them not be distressed . . . For when they live by the labour of their hands, as our fathers the apostles did, then they are really monks.' It is worth reflection that the only practice St Benedict explicitly commends as mon-

---

* This piece is a shortened version of an original article which appeared in *The Journal*, vol. 102, Autumn 1997.

astic in the whole of the Rule is that the monks should earn their living.

Yet work is not often seen as a part of the spiritual life. St Benedict meets this head on. For Benedict, idleness is the enemy because monks who do not work well will not pray well. Therefore he says, monks 'should have specified periods for manual labour as well as for prayerful reading'. Work is given a protected place in the monastic timetable, just as much as prayer and the *Opus Dei*. This is quite a radical position. The force of St Benedict's commendation of work is not simply that it is another good monastic practice, but there is something about work which sums up the goals of monastic, and hence of Christian life.

Toil and trouble

Today there is a large degree of confusion about the purpose and value of work. For many, the word 'work' is synonymous with 'toil'. There are two opposing tendencies, which to some degree are present in everyone. One is to minimize work as much as possible, 'clocking' on and off, with little regard for what is done in between or the sense of purpose in it. The other is the workaholic, who cannot stop, who stays late at work, or even brings it home at weekends. Work becomes a person's life. It would be unwise to rhapsodize about the supreme Christian value of work unless we understand that work for many is a kind of trap into either futility or hectic pursuit of rewards that there is little time to enjoy.

The issue can be put very simply. Many people feel alienated from their work. While some individuals have work which is fulfilling, many more feel no connection with the actual work they do and drudge away at something whose only direct bearing on their lives is that it provides them, if they are lucky, with the means to survive and perhaps raise children. Others feel alienated because the process of working for gain can itself be dehumanizing. People who do rotten jobs, or none at all, are easily seen as inferior, and easily see themselves as inferior. There is also a third level of alienation, which gives some clue to a way forward. It is a curious phenomenon of social history that at some point work became something one went out to do. We talk of domestic work, but it is not seen in the same way as, say, ploughing a field or brokering a deal. The trouble with this division is that we end up with a very artificial conception of what work is. It is seen as something which earns money from 'outside' and is judged by what it brings in, whether to the family or society as a whole. The worker is also judged in the same way. The focus is on *what* is done and for whom. We have to look instead at *who* is doing it.

The Work of God

If we wish to arrive at a Christian understanding of work, we have to begin with the basic facts of the faith. Work can easily become bound up with judgements about status. By contrast, St Paul's letter to the Philippians gives us a hymn about Christ, who though in the form of God, accepted the human state and became obedient even to the shameful death of a criminal. The Word became flesh and dwelt among us. Everything is changed by this, including our work.

To get the right view of work, we have to get the right view of humanity. Instead of valuing certain types of work above others, we should think that each is being done by a human being, created and loved by God. If we really want to know what is valuable, we should look at what Christ did. Having found him performing simple and humble tasks at the carpenter's bench, we have to ask more searching questions about our value judgements.

What is work, seen in the context of God's revelation in Christ? There are ambiguities in the way that Christians talk about work. On the one hand, Genesis 1 depicts God as working for six days to create the world and implies that human work is a reflection of that divine toil. On the other hand, work is seen as a consequence of the Fall, a part of Adam's curse in Genesis 2. One approach gives us the much-derided 'work ethic', while the other leaves little room for seeing value in anything we do. There are two important points to note here. The first is that the problem is not with work itself, but the way we regard it. It is not our power to work which has resulted in today's sorry mess, but our tendency to use that power to do things other than love and serve the God who gave it. The correct understanding of work therefore is not to be found in socio-economic analyses, but in an examination of the human condition itself. The second point is found in these words from the Prologue to St Benedict's Rule:

> The labour of obedience will bring you back to him from whom you had drifted through the sloth of disobedience . . . Seeking his workman in a multitude of people, the Lord calls out to him and lifts his voice . . . (Prologue, first and fourth paragraphs)

What we might be tempted to see as a necessary evil or as a punishment is in fact the means used by God for our salvation. There is an ascetical quality to work in that it involves (often reluctant) effort. But the deeper point is that the incarnation of the Word has given us a gospel of work, the first tenet of which is that work has value precisely because it is done by human beings. Jesus slaving away at the carpenter's bench can encourage us to plod on with our column of figures or heap of bricks. However, the fact that it was God who was doing it changes everything; that apparently pointless drudge is given eternal value because God bothered to do it. Whatever we do in our God-given capacity for action can be grace-bearing since we may do it as human beings fully restored to the full image of God who took on our nature. Perhaps this seems too grand a vision of the daily round of the office or factory, but we must bear in mind *who* is doing that daily grind: a human person made in the image of God.

To know what an authentically human life looks like, we have to look at Christ. The incarnation of the Son of God ended in agony at Calvary. The central mystery of our redemption is that it comes through suffering and death. Just as significant as the life of God in Christ is the death of God in Christ. We have to set the glossy picture of work as participation in God's creative power against the starker vision of work as part of the sufferings of the body of Christ. Here we find reflected the barren nature of so much social life and exchange. The difference for Christian workers is that they accept their burden in the same spirit as Christ did. That spirit was one of saving love and such faith in God that the issue of that death was resurrection. Christians are meant to transform society and that is done by participation in its woes in faith and hope. Work we are reluctant to do, or the unwelcome idleness of unemployment or destitution, are part of what God has taken to himself on the cross. Idleness is the enemy of the soul because it springs from the conviction that God is not found in those things that bore or hurt us. It prevents us from accepting those burdens in the redeeming spirit of Christ. As such, work, whether it be designing planes or washing dishes, is part of the 'labour of obedience' which brings us back to God, just as much as the daily round of prayer and *lectio*.

Laurence McTaggart

Perseverance

Choices cause consequences. As one leaves the centre of Sydney the road forks. Going to the left up King's Street can lead eventually to Melbourne; continuing straight ahead one may find oneself in Perth: two very different cities separated by over 3,000 km. People beginning a journey need to be clear about their goal or they may find themselves in a very different place from what they had hoped. In the Rule of St Benedict, Chapter 72, Benedict contrasts the bitter zeal that makes a barrier to God's grace and the good zeal that opens us to divine and human love. Zeal, or perseverance, can be a two-edged sword. Constantly on our journey we need to ask ourselves how our spiritual disciplines and practices are furthering our journey to the Kingdom of God.

Consider the contrast between two monastics I have known. Sister A and Brother B have both been exemplary in their monastic observance, both contributed greatly to the physical well-being of their communities – yet the contrast in spirit is stark. Sr A suffered greatly towards the end of her life – changes in religious practice undermined her belief in God, her rigid personality kept her emotionally distant from her community. Did anyone grieve at her passing? – who knows, nothing showed but relief. In contrast, Br B is not only at the heart of his community, but also the bearer of God's life far beyond. His funeral will be a celebration of life in the midst of many tears.

What made the difference? The disciplines they chose to feed the life of faith. The only personal practice of Sr A that I know of is significant: each day she made her bed the same way as an expression of her Vow of Stability. No, don't laugh. There is a good lesson here. An ordered woman, she wanted to offer all to God, even the small things. So far so good. But she focused on what came easily, baptized her own preferences, and did not leave herself open to God's love and the demands of others.

Br B's actions seem to point to a decision made early in his monastic life to never let pass an act of charity he could possibly do. Thus open to God's providence and to serving others, he radiates equanimity and joy. Significantly he is also a most astute, if most kind, judge of character.

We all need practices to feed the life of faith and Benedictine spirituality provides a rich variety of resources: the work of God, *lectio divina*, prayer, work, hospitality, etc. At differing stages of life these resources will sustain our faith in differing ways. Discerning what is appropriate at any point in time is a challenge, but necessary if we are to run the way of God's commandments with joyful hearts.

In the midst of our first enthusiasm, we need to take stern stock of ourselves and embrace a disciplined spirituality. Chesterton has said that we inveigh against the sins we are least likely to commit. Unless we can recognize our genuine weakness we become sadly lost like Sr A. In this the comments of others on our personalities can be so helpful. If talkative, we could develop our listening skills, if naturally withdrawn, become sociable, if moody, emotional self-discipline works wonders, if reserved, play may be the challenge we need. Rarely will we overturn who God has made us to be but rather with balance we can flourish to God's glory.

Such early challenges are relatively easy to discern. The real difficulty comes further on the journey when we are called to negotiate the times and seasons that are the natural part of growth. Dramatic conversion is rarely the stuff of the journey and often it takes time before we realize we are on the wrong road. How can we recognize such? First, a sense of drudgery pervades our life. Notice this is not difficulty or suffering – both means by which God can foster growth – but rather a sense that we are not getting anywhere. Our prayers seems routine and we feel disengaged from others. This malaise can be good. It is as though God is letting us run out of petrol in the hope that we must stop and ask direction. Again, at this time, the comments of others can be enlightening. Once I had a call to change from a passing remark of a shopkeeper – nothing said unkindly but an observation that brought me up and made me reconsider the balance of my life.

At such times we need to reassess our lives in the light of the two great Commandments of Jesus, using the resources of our Benedictine spirituality. We who have prayed much may be called to shift the balance to service, we who have been hospitable may be called to withdraw in silent prayer, we who have been still may be called to study. The purpose of this testing is to make us sensitive to the Spirit at work in our hearts and so be schooled to love God and others more creatively.

Over time, the decisions we make and the practices we embrace form us, hopefully into Christ. Shaped by his Gospel and supported by others we may persevere to the fullness of everlasting life in the Kingdom of God.

Kym Harris OSB

The Vows

The Second Vatican Council's teaching about religious life in the Constitution on the Church starts with a discussion of the three evangelical counsels: chastity, poverty and obedience. The same is true of Pope John Paul II's Apostolic Exhortation 'Vita consecrata'.

The Rule of St Benedict never speaks of the evangelical counsels as such. However, St Benedict certainly believed that monks were called to chastity, poverty and obedience. In Chapter 33 he gives a fine description of the three evangelical counsels when he writes that 'no one may presume to give, receive or retain anything . . . especially since monks may not have the free disposal even of their own bodies and wills'.

The monk does not own property, does not have the free disposition of his body, and is not allowed to follow his own will: these are the three renunciations involved in the evangelical counsels of poverty, chastity and obedience.

When modern writers say that all religious profess the evangelical counsels, they are using a formula which did not emerge until several hundred years after St Benedict wrote. However, what St Benedict says in Chapter 33 reminds us that the three evangelical counsels are closely related to each other. When religious say that they have given up the right to possess property, as well as control of the body and of the will, this is another way of saying that they have given up everything: if you have given up your body, will and possessions, there is nothing left for you to own. That is why we can say that religious are dedicated totally and unreservedly to the service of God, out of love for him. That is what the evangelical counsels involve, and that is also what St Benedict calls for from his monks.

St Benedict says that newcomers spend a year as novices. Modern Church law requires that they then spend at least three years in temporary vows – that is, commitment for a period of time, to allow for a longer period of training and discernment. At the end of this period, they may make profession for life. This is what St Benedict describes in Chapter 58 of his Rule.

St Benedict writes that the candidate 'comes before the whole community in the oratory and promises stability, fidelity to monastic life and obedience'.

This promise is central to the commitment made by the monk, and it is helpful to explore the meaning of this promise, though it would be a mistake to try and define each of the three expressions in precise legal terms.

'Fidelity to monastic life' is an attempt to translate the Latin words *conversatio morum*. The meaning of this term has foxed scholars and commentators for years. One way of approaching it is to see it as the core element in the monastic commitment, and to examine what that commitment is. Cassian tells us that the monk's ultimate aim is to come to the Kingdom of God, and that his immediate goal is purity of heart, without which we shall never attain our ultimate aim.[1] A good way of describing *conversatio morum* is that it is the monk's commitment to pursuing this goal, through adopting the monastic programme of asceticism and prayer, as well as the monastic structure of life which is designed to support that programme.

If *conversatio morum* is the core of the monk's commitment, 'stability' and 'obedience' give more precision to the Benedictine way of leading the monastic life. 'Stability' implies perseverance, sticking to the programme once undertaken, 'faithfully observing his (God's) teaching in the monastery until death' (Prologue). Obedience recognizes the need for guidance. The Benedictine is a cenobite, serving 'under a rule and an abbot' (Chapter 1).

A mediaeval commentator, Bernard of Monte Cassino, thought that the threefold promise Benedict asks of his monks distinguishes them from the three other types of monk we find in Chapter 1.[2] Bernard wrote that Benedictine monks are stable, unlike gyrovagues, who wander from one place to another; they are under a superior, unlike hermits, who have been tried and tested and no longer need the guidance of a superior; they seek a true monastic way of life, unlike sarabaites, who have no rule and whose characters are as soft as lead.

While St Benedict may not have thought in these terms, it is quite a useful way of looking at the promise he asks of his monks. If someone wants to be a member of a Benedictine community, he needs to know that stability, conversatio morum and obedience are the ground rules for community membership.

However, it would be a mistake to see profession simply in terms of accepting the rules of a club. It is, above all, an act of self-dedication to God, made out of love since, as St Benedict tells us (Chapter 5), it is love that impels the monk to pursue everlasting life. And this act of self-dedication is vividly expressed in the ritual St Benedict prescribes when a monk is professed.

The monk, after making his promise, draws up a written document and places this on the altar. When we celebrate the Mass, gifts of bread and wine are placed on the altar. These gifts are received by the Church and will be used exclusively for the honour and glory of God, as they are destined to become the Body and Blood of Christ. Like the bread and the wine, the monk's document is placed on the altar. It becomes a symbol of the monk's self-giving to the Lord. Monks, through making their profession, are totally dedicated to the honour and glory of God, and to his service.

Richard Yeo OSB

Notes

1 Cassian, *Conferences*, I, IV.
2 Bernard of Monte Cassino, *Expositio in Regulam*, c. 58.

Hospitality

An acquaintance once said to me, 'You are wrong when you say that hospitality is at the centre of the Christian Church. It isn't hospitality,' she insisted, 'it's fear.' The woman, a Catholic convert, was responding to a chapter in my book, *The Cloister Walk*, in which I talk about how monastic hospitality opened the doors of Christian faith to me, overcoming what had seemed insurmountable obstacles of doubt and dread, including the fear of a God who wants to punish me for being who I am.

The world could use more of the fear of the Lord, which is the first stage of wisdom, the healthy fear of wonder and reverence before a God who knows us better than we know ourselves and loves us anyway. But we would do well to let go of the narcissistic fear that makes us anxious under circumstances and with people we can't control. When misfortune strikes, and we fall victim to accident, illness, or the bad intentions of others, we can choose how to respond, either falling back on our own resources and withdrawing from a dangerous world, or remaining open to what God has placed before us. The latter, Benedict insists, is always our best response. Hospitality is a tool that keeps us focused, not on ourselves, but on 'the divine presence [that] is everywhere' (the Rule of St Benedict, Chapter 19). The stranger at our door may bring new dangers and temptations, or be an angel in disguise. But Benedict trusts that in the play of hospitality, in learning how to give and to receive that which we cannot truly give or earn, we will be brought closer to the mystery of the Incarnation.

It is remarkable that in the Rule, which is otherwise so humane and flexible, there is no leeway regarding hospitality: 'All guests who present themselves are to be welcomed as Christ' (Chapter 53, first paragraph). No wriggle room, no way out, no chance to respond to a visitor's demands by saying, in an exasperated tone, 'Can't you see we're trying to run a monastery here?' The monk I know who did say that to a guest asking one too many questions about monastic life spent the next day apologizing to her, and the next ten years telling the story on himself.

Benedict places his chapter on the reception of guests late in the Rule, after he has established the sort of place a monastery is to be. This is proper, for only those who are truly at home in themselves can offer genuine hospitality, which is not controlling or manipulative, but welcomes us as we are. For the guest the most refreshing thing about monastic hospitality is that it does not seek to turn you into a 'monklet', a celibate, or a Roman Catholic, but guides you in honouring your own vows, in my case as a married Presbyterian lay preacher and deacon.

Unlike commercial hospitality, which provides a comforting sameness, monastic hospitality is always surprising, as it liberates guests to discern their true needs. People who go to a monastery to rest begin working hard instead, writing a poem for the first time in years, or composing a conciliatory letter to an estranged friend. But a pilgrim who comes prepared to work may find it impossible. On my first retreat, when I complained to an elderly monk that I had been too sleepy to even begin the spiritual books I had intended to read, he said, 'Maybe sleep is the most spiritual thing you can do right now.'

Benedict demands a radical hospitality from monks, but he also knows that they need to keep some time and space reserved for themselves alone: 'The kitchen for the abbot and guests ought to be separate, so that guests – and monasteries are never without them – need not disturb the brothers when they present themselves at unpredictable hours' (Chapter 53, fifth paragraph). This is not fussiness or exclusivity but a wise acknowledgement of a deep psychological truth. People who give so much of themselves that they lose their own identity are not truly hospitable, and neither the monastery nor the pilgrim is well served if monks use guests as a means of escaping dull routine, or an unhappy community life. In *Seeking God* Esther de Waal reminds us that monastic hospitality has two simple ends: Did they see Christ in us? Did we see Christ in them?

To Benedict, the mundane hospitality we offer others has a divine purpose, and he uses a judgement text in Matthew to underscore this point: 'All guests who present themselves are to be welcomed as Christ, for he himself will say, "I was a stranger and you welcomed me"' (Chapter 53, first paragraph). Christ will recognize is in the new creation, as he has already encountered us in this one. The Incarnation is God's hospitality to us, a means of welcoming us not only as friends, but as family. We, in turn, are called to be fully present to one another now, and to live our lives keeping in mind St Paul's admonition to 'Welcome one another . . . just as Christ has welcomed you, for the glory of God' (Rom. 15:7).

Kathleen Norris

Bibliography

de Waal, Esther, *Seeking God: The Way of St Benedict*, Collins Fount, London, 1984. New Edition, Canterbury Press, Norwich, 1999.
Norris, Kathleen, *The Cloister Walk*, Lion, Oxford, 1999.